Sunrise within You

Achieving Significance in Life

Sunrise within You

Achieving Significance in Life

Pritam Kumar Goswami

Notion Press

5 Muthu Kalathy Street, Triplicane,

Chennai - 600 005

First Published by Notion Press 2013

Hardcase ISBN: 979-8-89475-733-9
Paperback ISBN: 978-9-38341-635-6

"If a man has not discovered something that he will die for, he is not fit to live."

- Martin Luther King

Preface

When you start looking for your worth, your abilities, efficiency, potential and capabilities, your own answer to this could be a bit daunting. All sorts of questions will occur to you and you may not be quite sure what the answers are or even how to find out what they are.

This book – "Sunrise within you" is aimed to give you these answers. This book will surely enlighten and encourage you to make a positive and determined approach to your valuable life, personality and your own worth.

Over the last ten years I have travelled the length and breadth of the world visiting the top schools, colleges, professional institutes, villages, hospitals, banks, welfare associations and companies lecturing on balanced life, career, relationships, goals, self awareness etc. I have always subscribed to the philosophy, that one must know what he is capable of doing before taking any step to take his life anywhere.

This book shall prove to be an invaluable tool for every person wanting a positive change or say a positive start in life. It will help you to focus and prioritize ways to lead a successful and prosperous life, one that will be every bit as fulfilling and rewarding as you deserve.

Starting with how to search your true self, the book goes on to help you to understand the need to explore the inner hidden potentials. It also guides you in your relationships through various principles and then takes you through the rigours of challenges that life throws. Not only personality, the books actually highlights the overall development and consistent growth of an individual in various areas in great details to facilitate your familiarization with them.

The Changing scenario with its implications is analysed so that in making your decision you stand on a firm base of awareness of the present and future.

In helping you to establish your priorities, the book also focuses on the intricacies of working the wrong way and the pitfalls to avoid.

In addition, I have sought to focus on aspects of self-development with the underlying feeling that 'your attitude determines your altitude', and 'whatever the mind of a man conceives and heart believes you can achieve'. Awareness, knowledge and skills give us more options in life, possessions of them allows us to live fuller lives shaping events rather than simply reacting.

I have tried to suggest that personality growth, communication skills and traits like integrity, temperance, patience, modesty and positivity are character building blocks. Along with other skills and qualifications these character building blocks have been and will continue to be the pre-requisites for success and growth in life.

The power of sub-conscious mind is again another topic which will provide loads of energy to your 'self' in putting much more efforts in working hard towards the definite goal. 'Accepting failures', 'Stress management' and 'Values & social ethics' are such topics which will provide a new outlook to your vision and widen the horizons of your understandings.

I am indebted to my wife 'Vineeta' and my sons 'Vedant' & 'Parth' for all unconditional support in coming out with this wonderful creation. I am privileged to be son of my mom and dad who gave me best of the learning in life and always motivated me to do my best. I owe my father and mother for all motivation, support and blessings.

I am thankful to my partners Mr. Anil Jain, Mr. Sushil Aggarwal, Mr. Pawan Lalpuria & Dr. Ajay Sharma to help me attaining maturity and making me learn invaluable life lessons. Many of such lessons came through my mentor Mr. Nirmal Parekh who inculcated the instinct to come out with the bundle of thoughts in form of a book.

I am thankful to one of the best life schools of the world "Junior Chamber International". It helped me re-inventing myself and optimizing my performance. I thank Mr. K.Vallabhdas the patron and past national president of Junior Chamber International India for giving me leadership opportunities which in fact helped me gathering lots of experience and exposure.

I am also thankful to Amrita Panjwani & Monika for helping me putting my thoughts on the paper.

For the publication of the book I feel a sense of gratitude towards Notion Press for publishing "Sunrise within You."

Last but most important. I thank God for all blessings and this task was almost impossible without his being the head and controller of my life. I am truly blessed.

I am sure that 'Sunrise within you' will certainly bring sizeable difference to your life, A new dawn in your life.

Pritam Kumar Goswami

Contents

1

A Discovery Within You

In life, there are people better than you; there are people worst than you. But there will never be one who is "YOU"! Stay Special!!!

I have a firm belief that each one of us is born with a unique purpose in life to fulfil, because nature doesn't create anybody without a reason.

Most people in this world lead mechanical life. They get up in the morning, get ready and go to work. They come back and eat again, watch T.V. and go to sleep. When they were children they wanted to grow big, when they grew they got married and started thinking for their children and other responsibilities. Some years later their children got married and it was all over for them. If someone asks them nobody will be able to tell one single mission or purpose for which they lived for.

Do you have a mission in your life? Do you want to make your life meaningful? Do you want to be remembered by the world? Do you want to leave a legacy? Do you want to become an example for others? Start thinking about the purpose of your life, start getting into yourself and discover your true self.

The journey of finding the purpose of life starts with discovery within. Unless we know who we are, we can't guide ourselves. Out of billions of people living in the world only few thousands have done something exceptional and created an impact. They knew about their strengths and had belief in their abilities. They had a vision and mission to achieve. Amidst all the challenges and adversities in life they could proceed further because they knew what is to be accomplished.

All great accomplishments in the world have been attained by ordinary humans only. Don't you think if they can do it you can also do it?

When we are born we are fresh and not biased with negative thoughts or any kind of inferiority. Slowly and gradually when we start growing we start developing our perceptions towards the life. Most of us fail to know our capabilities and potentials and never use them in our life time. We even don't know that we have certain capabilities. That's the reason why most of the people are not able to do what they could have done, because they never believed that they could do it. They never had awareness and knowledge about their own personality. That's why most of us fail to achieve significance in our life.

Somebody has truly said "People live like in this world as if they will never go, and when they go it looks as if they never lived." This applies to majority of people and you may be one of them.

Before going further I would like to ask you the following questions:

What is the mission of your life?

Have you done justice with your potential fully?

Are you aware of changes you want to bring in your personality?

Are you growing towards goodness, everyday?

Are you ready to face future challenges?

If you want to make your life meaningful, if you want to be different from others you need to discover the real you. Start doing it from today itself, because "There will never be a better time to start doing right things."

Believe me you are the best and you are capable of doing what you desire. Warrant buffet rightly said, "***There will never be a better you than you.***" You are unique, you are special and you are different from every one. Then why don't you take a step forward to know yourself better and start making the difference.

Self Image Builds the Foundation for Your Success

Every person lives with three kinds of images. The first one is what people think of you, like what kind of person you are. The second image is what you think about yourself, which is known as Self-image of yours and the third is the actual image about which you may not be aware of.

Self image is a mental picture of yours stored in your mind which makes you feel that what kind of person you are. The self image affects your feelings about how much you can do.

Remember:

"An individual's self-image is the core of his personality. It affects every aspect of human behavior: the ability to learn, the capacity to grow and change . . . ."

An interesting quality of the self-image is that it doesn't have to be true. Yes, it doesn't have to be true.

But, having a correct and positive self-image is necessary to produce desired outcome in every walk of life right from the childhood. So, develop a positive self-image

. . . A strong, positive self-image is the best possible preparation for success in life.

- Joyce Brothers

If you carry a good self-image your self confidence is bound to grow and you will have belief in your abilities. You must have seen many people in your vicinity who despite a lot of talents and skills fail. The reason is pretty obvious. The never knew about their hidden potential and abilities. They carried negative self image about themselves.

Therefore, if you wish to capitalize on all your inner strengths then you need to correct the self image. You need to believe that you can do it, you can succeed in business, you can earn lots of money, you can score more marks etc. The positive self image always helps you gaining self confidence and overcome all fears and inferiorities.

Three Stages of Self Awareness

a) I Know What I know: When you are aware of skills, knowledge & Competencies which we posses like I know I can speak French, I know I can drive a car, I know I can solve a mathematics problem etc.

b) I Know What I Don't know: When you are aware of skills, knowledge and competencies which you don't posses like I know that I can't fly an airplane, I know that I can't speak Japanese, I know that I can't cook, I can't control my anger etc.

c) The third dimension is most critical one and most of us are suffering because we are ignorant about this it goes like this "I don't know what I don't know" means you are not aware about the fact that what's lacking in you and if you don't know this, you never try to achieve the same. Therefore creating awareness about the third dimension is extremely important for becoming an extra ordinary individual, to compete with the world and to upgrade with the changing times.

Be Different from Others

BE YOURSELF: An original is always worth more than a copy.

The population of world is in billions but we never come across two such persons who are replica of each other in every sense except in cinemas. That's next to impossible to find two such persons because they don't exist. The billions of people who are living on earth have their own set of thoughts, their own style of working and living, their own talents, their own pluses and minuses. You are good at one thing which other person may not be and vice versa. Therefore you need to identify how you are different from others, what is your actual personality, what are unique features of your personality. Without knowing any such things you try to follow others blindly i.e. everybody is trying to be photocopy of others but the same success formula can't be applied to everyone.

At bottom every man knows well enough that he is a unique being, only once on this earth; and by no extraordinary chance will such a marvelously picturesque piece of diversity in unity as he is, ever be put together a second time.

- Friedrich Nietzsche

If you want to achieve something exceptional you have to find out in yourself what differentiates you from others. The unique and exclusive characteristic has to be discovered. Thus, be yourself and, be different from the world.

Only by being 'different' from others you can make the 'difference' provided you are 'aware about that difference'.

Every man of genius sees the world at a different angle from his fellows.

- Havelock Ellis

Be daring, be different, be impractical, be anything that will assert integrity of purpose and imaginative vision against the play-it-safe, the creatures of the commonplace, the slaves of the ordinary.

- Cecil Beaton

Understanding Internal & External Affairs

The most important part of self awareness is making an inventory of your resources i.e. understanding your strengths and using them as trump card in life. But at the same time you can't ignore your weaknesses, you have to identify things which are creating hindrance in your way. Though it's difficult to completely overcome all weaknesses but of course they can be minimized or managed in such a way that they don't negate the effect of your strengths.

Similarly with the set of strengths you possess you may confront with many good opportunities which are available to you and by having those strengths you can avail those chances. But again you need to be aware about those chances. As we all know that we are living in the world which is full of challenges and nothing is static. Therefore there are lots of challenges in every field be it sports, business, education or jobs. These challenges and threats are to be understood well and taken care of well in advance, so the impact is minimal and not devastating.

"Capitalize your strengths, suppress the weaknesses, encash the opportunities, and be aware of threats. "

Do You Know Your Core Competence?

Now let's talk about core competence. What's the secret behind success of companies like Reliance, Microsoft, Sony, Mittal Arcelor. The answer is clear; all these companies identified their core area and worked on that only. The backward integration approach of Reliance, The brand image and proactive approach of Microsoft and Sony and the taking over sick units strategy of Mittal's are few examples of core competence. They have tremendous amount of expertise on their core areas that's why they are market leaders in their respective fields.

Each one of us is also having some or the other talent, skill and some core qualities. First you need to identify that core competence, make it a foundation and then act aggressively. No matter what's your background, no matter how do you appear, no matter you are less intelligent than others but if you know about the special feature of your personality that makes you unique and that differentiates you from others you can certainly create miracles in life.

So, if you want to be valued, find out your core-competence and excel in it. And,

What you want to excel, make it your habit.

Don't be Externally Driven

"The only real valuable thing is intuition."

- Albert Einstein

Once I conducted a survey of 100 people of more than 60 years of age covering all class of people like rich, poor, educated, illiterate, man, woman, urban and rural. I was keen in knowing about their experiences of their lives as a whole, the way they lived their life and their contentment levels. A surprising fact emerged at the end. Most of the people were not satisfied with their life styles, decisions they made and the way they spent their years. It was an evident observation that most of them could not do what they desired or dreamt. But because of indirect force and under pressure they did what others expected or forced them to do. It happens with many of us right from our childhood. We are pressurized to follow certain things, to opt for certain things. We are that much conditioned with this habit that till our old age we keep on doing things which have never been our desire.

Therefore being an internally driven person is the key to explore your core competence and this is the only way by which you can search your true self.

Forget about what people have to say but do what your inner conscience permits.

"A man cannot be comfortable without his own approval."

"Don't listen to friends when the Friend inside you says 'Do this.'"

Develop a Passion for What You Do or Vice Versa

We have a perception about successful people that they must have done a Herculean task or must have carried out rigorous efforts to reach their existing levels. But one of the most important factors to their success is that they had passion for what they did. You can see people working day and night with tremendous amount of zeal, excitement and not getting tired. In contrast it happens with many of us that by keeping ourselves exposed to continued work for consecutive hours we get exhausted. This has been proved by medical science that if we do something with a great internal interest a passion for work is developed subconsciously which results in good efficiency at work.

The renowned scientist 'Thomas Alva Edison' was once interviewed by a journalist, a surprising question was asked to him. The journalist asked "Mr. Edison you have around 1000 patents to your credit, I have heard that scientists go mad only in couple of inventions how could you work so much?" He mildly replied, "Look gentleman! I never worked even for a single minute. What I did is I enjoyed and had lots of fun."

Similarly the tennis legend 'Pete Sampras' once told that I am very fortunate that I chose tennis as my career because I am in love with it.

It gives lesson of life to us and the message is very clear. "Do what you love. If you don't have that choice, then develop love for what you are already doing. If you want to double your success rate and want more results out of your performance you need to develop a lot of passion and love for what you do, you should feel happiness and thrill while carrying out your task. It definitely leads towards excellence.

Passion/Enthusiasm is one of the most powerful engines of success. When you do a thing, do it with all your might. Put your whole soul into it. Stamp it with your own personality. Be active, be energetic and faithful, and you will accomplish your object. Nothing great was ever achieved without passion/enthusiasm."

- Ralph Waldo Emerson

"Without work, all life goes rotten. But when work is soulless, life stifles and dies."

- Albert Camus

Self Confidence

If you believe you can do it you will definitely accomplish that. If you think you can't you won't be able to finish the simplest of the tasks. We have seen many ordinary people doing extraordinary things. But all that was the outcome of positive self confidence. If you are not confident enough for something you will try to avoid doing that. By doing this you will lose the opportunity of learning. We are here to make our mistakes and die our lessons learnt.

The reason for lack of self-confidence is due to lack of self belief, fear of failures and they may come from a negative self image or sense of inferiority. When you are not exposed to a new situation, you will have lots of reservations and that will lead you to have a lack of belief in yourself, in your decisions & in your actions too.

"Jo til mein hai tel, jo jagmag mein hai aag,
tera Sai hai tere andar, jag sake to jaag"
(Hindi saying by poet-saint Kabir)

"Sesame seeds contain oil within; Flint stones hold potential sparks. Your potential lies within you, awake to this fact."

Please note that sesame seeds need to be crushed to produce oil... that flint stones need to struck against each other to create a spark of fire… similarly we need to realize the potential within us.

Duniya se to bahut mil chuka, Khud se bhi to mil,

Jis din tu khud se mil lega, Payega manzil.

(We spend our entire life in understanding the outer world, and ignore the strongest and mighty inner self of ours. The day when we will take notice of it, we will outperform the whole world.)

Try to explore that facet of yourself which is highly confident and believes in you, which has positive self-image because self-image is the platform from where all our actions flow. It is the image on our internal mirrors. Therefore, to change the results, you must change the negative blueprint you have created over the time.

Since repetition created the state of your current image, it will also take repetition to change your state of mind from unhealthy to healthy. This is where most of the people breakdown. You simply don't muster the stamina or the faith to repeat the right behaviour and action long enough to create a healthy self-image, that can lead you to become more than you think you are.

You must build and modify your self-image through positive auto suggestions…..means those words and pictures that trigger the positive images to give you the power to move in the right direction. Over time, these new directions lead you to feel better about yourself, enhance your character, and release within you the power to outperform and be your best.

You need to change your thinking pattern and start moving from:

From	**To**
I think	I will
I will try	I can
I might	I know
May be	Definitely
I hope so	Okay
I don't know	Fantastic
Let me see	Great
Possibly	Always
Perhaps	Absolutely

"What the mind can conceive, the man can achieve".

There is a Hero
If you look inside your heart
You don't have to be afraid of what you are
There is an answer if you reach into your soul
And that sorrow that you know will melt away
And then a hero comes along with the
strength to carry on
And you cast your fears aside & you know
you can survive
So when you feel like hope is gone, look inside you
& be strong
And you will finally see the truth
That the hero lies in you!
(A song by Mariah Carrey)

Believe in Your Own Worth

Even the best needles are not sharp at both ends.
- Chinese Proverb

About few hundred years ago an old widow lady was living in a small town with her young son about 22 years of age. The son never studied, never earned, never cared for mother rather involved in all anti social activities. People in town were generally afraid of him. Mother was too much concerned and worried about the future of her son, she tried to give him wisdom but failed in every such attempt. Once a renowned saint visited the town and stayed there for few days. Saint used to spend some time with people of the town, listening to their personal problems and guiding them to resolve their problems.

The old lady with an intention to help her son coming on the right track and understanding the value of life took him to the saint. The lady said "Sir, he is my son and doing nothing, he has no concern for his future and known to be notorious in the society. I don't want him to be an extra ordinary person in his life instead I want him to be a normal and self dependent guy so when I die he can feed himself without hurting anybody."

The saint replied "Look, I have no solution to your problem rather I can see that there is no future of your son because he is going to die after 7 days." Both, the lady and her son got stunned listening to the words of the saint. The lady started crying on the spot, and returned back to home with that grief in the heart. The son was still in a state of shock and unable to utter a single word throughout the day. Whole day he was sitting in one corner of the house and went to sleep in the night. Whole night he could not sleep with a fear and tension that very soon he is going to die. He could not believe that his life will soon come to an end. While thinking all this during the sleepless night he started realizing his mistakes and all his deeds which caused harms to many people. He didn't want that people will be cursing his mother after his death. To minimise the damage he thought of going to as many as people he can and saying sorry for his wrong deeds. Next morning he moved out of his home and whole day he met many of the people living in his neighbourhood talking to them, saying sorry and requesting them to forgive him. He returned back in the late evening and had nice and relaxed sleep. He was too relaxed as if he has got relieved from lots of burden. Third day he again moved out of his house with another motive and came back in the evening. He called his mom, took the few coins out from his pocket and said, "Mom look, you wanted me to earn all through my life, for the first time in my life I have earned this money through honesty and hard work." Mother again got emotional, because she wanted her son to be a good person and he was trying to be a good person when a very few days of his life were remaining.

Today is the seventh and last day of his life. He goes to his mother and says "Mom today is the last day of my life and we will not be meeting again, therefore I will spend the whole day with you." While saying this he was cool, calm and composed as if he doesn't have any fear of dying. He spends the whole day with his mother and returns to his room in the evening. He was constantly staring at the clock, waiting for midnight, when seventh day was to end and his soul will depart. When it was almost 12 in the midnight he closed his eyes with anxiety, after almost 15 minutes he felt to be in conscious state and realized that he is still alive. He amidst uncertainty went to his bed and could not sleep the whole night with a tension that why didn't he die? In the early morning he rushed to the saint and asked "Sir, you said that I am going to die after seven days, I somehow made myself ready for that but I didn't die." The saint smiled a bit and said "My son, you must be thinking that the prediction I made seven days back was wrong. In fact I was all correct. The person who came to me seven days back has already died. The person sitting in front of me is a newly born person, who knows how to accept his mistakes, how to care, how to say sorry and also understands the value of his life." Yes my son this is your new birth and your life starts now. That young man later on became a famous saint and preacher.

Many of us lead our life without understanding any worth of it. We keep on spending our days without any purpose. The day you realize that you have very limited time to spend and within that limited time frame you have to accomplish certain things, your approach towards life changes drastically. Your efforts will enhance automatically and you will start having amazing results.

You might have born many years ago but your life only starts when you consciously start endeavours to make certain things happen.

We may have some flaws in our personality but we have many inherent qualities too. We must understand that life is a treasurer and one day you are going to lose this treasure. Live it to your best and leave the legacy.

Ring the bells that still can ring
Forget your perfect offering.
There is a crack in everything,
that's how the light gets in.

- Leonard Cohen

The imperfections of a man, his frailties, his faults, are just as important as his virtues. You can't separate them. They're wedded.

- Henry Miller

Learn Self-romancing....

At its core, Loving yourself simply means believing in your own indispensable worth. It is fostering a healthy sense of positive self-regard and admitting in your heart that you are a special creation of God. Loving yourself also means actively caring for every aspect of you. It shows up in every action you take, from putting on a sweater to protect yourself from a cold, to leave a job that does not fulfill you. It means accepting your own wants and needs and honoring them the exact same way you want your best friend to attend to you.

Remember that - Respecting, nurturing, honoring and cherishing yourself is your birth right.

If you are always fighting with yourself and feeding yourself thoughts that make you feel less valuable or not as important or attractive as other people, then you are suffering from Low Self-Esteem. Unfortunately, most people suffer from this, but the good news is, you can kick low self-esteem out of your life, inviting and living a high self-esteem instead.

All you are required to do is to make it with yourself; you will have to learn how to live happily with yourself, after accepting all of your flaws with grace, as if you are none other but your own beloved. You will have to take all the responsibility of your own, as if you are your own kid. You will have to teach and train yourself eventually to make yourself a person, which is respectable and lovable in your own eyes, as if you are your own mentor. But firstly you will have to accept, respect and love yourself for what you are.

Begin by becoming a best friend to yourself instead of an enemy. Look in the mirror and tell yourself that you do not feel sorry for yourself anymore (because you love yourself and you feel proud for your beloved in spite of all his/her flaws) and that you have the power and strength to feel and be happy, confident and successful, and you will do it because you are valuable and deserve it, just as anyone else would. Take notes of the positive things and the things you do like and admire about yourself.

Another essential thing you must remember is that you are different and unique and hold talents and qualities that no one else has and will never have, and that is something to take pride in and love about you. Concentrate on learning and knowing that you are special, loveable, capable and very much acceptable.

It all begins with accepting yourself, and you are the most important person to receive acceptance from. Once you have received a spokesperson approval and acceptance from yourself, everything and everyone else around you will do the same and follow.

Be aware of your self-talk (those things that you say to yourself inside your head). Speak to yourself in ways that are more kind, and less mean or abusive. Many of us have very harsh inner critics: When we make a mistake, this critical voice inside our head beats up on us, saying things like, "That was so stupid! ... I can't do anything right! ... What a loser!" We need to replace these negative messages with other, more positive ones. For example, "I made a mistake, that's okay, that is how I learn, I'll know better the next time." With awareness, over time, you can "catch yourself" when your self-talk is negative, and change the message to something more positive and "esteem-enhancing."

Don't just "catch yourself being wrong." "Catch yourself being right." In other words, don't just catch the voice of your inner critic, and stop it from beating up on you. When you do something well, or when you find yourself saying the right things to yourself or to others, be sure to reward yourself: acknowledge yourself verbally, give yourself a pat on the back, or treat yourself to something special.

Start self-romancing; means, tell yourself each day, "I am happy and successful" or "I am beautiful and bright" or "I love my body: I feel healthy and in balance" or "I am loving, caring, and worthy of love" or "I am powerful and self-confident" ...and whatever qualities you wish to be, and mean it. Even if, at first, you feel silly or uncomfortable repeating or reading these phrases, you may find that too soon you grow into and become these qualities. You may even realize that you embodied them all along; you just had not realized it.

So, go ahead. Love yourself. Be good to yourself. Treat yourself well. Replenish yourself. You will discover that, the more you love yourself, the more you will be able to give love to others - and the more others will want to be around you and give back to you. This is a win-win situation. Loving yourself will ultimately benefit the lives of others you encounter, as well as your own life.

Be with Yourself......

Just Imagine!

There's a person whom you love the most in your life.

These days, he needs you very much because he has loosened confidence in himself.

But you believe in him.

You very well know that he has a great potential and can be one of the greatest achievers.

And, you know him the best.

But now, if you are not going to do it for him, nobody else is going to do that.

Then what will you do?

You will help him to rise,

You will just appreciate him and show confidence in him because he needs this very much, ...and you'll make him happy with him and make him trust himself.

You will be his power; make him realize his own potential,

You will rate him the best even in the worst of his times,

So that he can rebuild the power in himself.

And you know what...

He is nobody else,

but **YOU**.

Yes, he is you.

So help and trust yourself.

Love yourself and be your own best friend forever like bff's.*

And just be with yourself always.

Stand like a pillar by your side.

And then,

The rest of the world will be set aside by your internal power and strength.

(*bff à best friends forever)

And remember one thing very clearly, the one who can't prove to be the best friend to one, can't prove to

be the same to anybody else. God has bestowed all of us with so many gifts to be happy and thankful to him. And first and foremost of such is our life, ourselves. So you are being given you at the first place to love. And the one who can't be with this person, who is none other but himself, can't make it with anybody else. And so is the saying – First and Last Love Is Self-Love.

You are Special!

Don't you think that you are continuously ignoring one thing and that is – YOU.

You too, are special…

In fact, you are 100% perfect as you are.

Most of us are struggling because we have ignored ourselves. We are perfect but don't realize it.

You can succeed by realizing that you already are a success. You are successful in spite of your mistakes and misfortunes and flaws.

You are special for being here. You know that but you sometimes forget.

Let me remind you again – You are special.

Exercise on Self Analysis

Here is a wonderful exercise on analyzing yourself and identifying your strengths and areas of improvement. Here are 30 important qualities which one must possess to be a great persona. You have to rate yourself on a scale from 0 to 10. Spend some 3-5 minutes on each quality by thinking about your behaviour in various situations in that particular context and then give the rating. Please be honest with yourself. If you are not honest to yourself you can't be honest with anybody else.

Qualities	**Rating (1 to 10)**
Hard Work	
Positive Attitude	
Go Getter	
Leadership	
Team Spirit	
Co-operation	
Sincerity	
Discipline	
Punctuality	
Passion	
Dedication	
Committed	
Trustworthiness	
Integrity	
Adaptability	
Confidence	
Creativity	
Courtesy	
Mental Toughness	
Sense of Humour	
Proactive	
Planning	
Empathy	
Cool Temperament	
Visionary	
Interpersonal Skills	
Patience	
Ambitious	
Curious	

(The above list is not exhaustive. You may add few more qualities while evaluating yourself)

After giving rating to abovementioned items, identify where you score 6 or more, these are your strengths and you have to capitalize on them to achieve your goals. If you score 5 or less, these are your areas of improvement. Now you will have clear idea about the homework you have to do to improve yourself.

Adding Value on Daily Basis

As a true and progressive human being you need to add value to yourself on daily basis. If you are the same person what you were few months back in terms of knowledge, skills and attitude you simply wasted those valuable months of your life which you not going to get back. Unless you are growing consistently, you are getting obsolete. If you stop learning and gaining new things you start dying. You need to introspect regularly about value additions to your personality and knowledge.

YOU can also do it

Give yourself a couple of minutes and think about extraordinary people in the world who are known as achievers. What was different in them and how you are different from them? Once I was listening to a speaker and stunned to hear one simple line. "If those achievers could do extraordinary things you can also do, they were also human beings and you are also human being". They were ordinary people before doing extraordinary tasks. You need to have self belief, if others can do you can also do.

"I would like to share my own example over here. I was an ordinary student till I finished my graduation in commerce. I never scored more than 60% marks in any standard up to my graduation. After graduation I decided to join professional

course of Chartered Accountancy. When I joined this course everyone was literally behind me and giving me an adverse opinion that I won't be able to do it. It's going to be too difficult for me and results are too less etc. Seriously speaking, I never thought that I won't be able to do that. I kept on studying and working towards my aim and within three years I completed my C.A. that too with 100% self studies. When I returned to my town 'Kota' I was interested in knowing the fate of other 16 students who were my batch mates and joined the same course. I was amazed to know that none of them could complete their course till that time. The interesting fact is that all of them were ahead of me in academic performance and one of them was State cum university topper in graduation. That day I realized, we can accomplish every such task which others are capable of doing. Don't get biased with your past performance. We perform poorly because we are not focused and have less faith in our abilities. I could do it because I didn't compare myself with others and I took the course with a mindset that I will complete it within designated time."

Who Says You Lack Self Confidence?

I generally ask in my seminars, "How many of you think that you lack self confidence? Be honest and raise your hands". Almost 70-80% participants raise their hands. I further ask "When and how did you come to know about this disease of yours? Whether some medical test revealed it, your horoscope tells it or you dreamt about this weakness of yours"? Most of them are speechless. Someone then replies "Well, when I was in school I had an opportunity to speak during annual function and the moment I reached on the stage I felt to be nervous and couldn't speak anything, then, I realized that I don't have self confidence".

Confidence is such a quality which is inherent and can't be obtained from outside. First you need to realize that you have it in. You feel nervous because you were never exposed to that situation. You simply need some preparation and practice. But most of us out of that nervousness correlate it with lack of confidence and start keeping it in the mind which always stays as a mental block and never allows you to act as confident person. Remember confidence is already there in you, just have belief and explore it.

Remember you are responsible for what you get in life, whether it's good or bad. You need to dig deep down in yourself to find real self of you. Instead of thinking about others introspect and create that awareness about your strengths and areas for improvement.

2

You And Your Inner Voice

(The Art of Positive Self Talk)

Have you ever observed where you saw yourself in an upset state of mind? You know that you are into botheration for few weeks. Then after few days or weeks you suddenly realize that the matter which was bothering you doesn't really matter a lot or may be, you talked to close one of yours about botheration and felt much better afterwards. Probably your friend said something to you which made you think differently about the problem and that changed your whole attitude towards that feeling.

Here the experience in changing of the feeling exhibits a crucial principle. Changing the way you think will change the way you feel. Things go wrong at times, people let us down, we make mistakes, failures occur and disappointments happen. Whether or not we get upset about it, and how upset we become, depends largely on the way we think about those situations. Sometimes we can make ourselves feel pretty miserable even when our situation is not that bad, simply by thinking in a negative, self-defeating way.

What's Your Inner Voice?

In our daily lives we are regularly thinking about various situations and interpreting them differently in different circumstances. A constant discussion goes inside our head which finally generates a feeling. The feeling is the result of how we perceive that situation? We may call it inner voice or Self-talk, and it includes our conscious and unconscious thoughts, beliefs and presumptions. Many of our internal discussions are OK like "I have to prepare for tomorrow's meeting, or I am really looking forward for my sister's marriage. However, some of our self-talk are negative or illusionary or may be self defeating viz. I can't win that deal, or I can't do well in this subject.

Negative Self-discussion

Negative self-discussions often make us to feel bad, and to experience upsetting emotions such as hurt, anger, frustration, confusion, depression or anxiety. It can also make us behave in a self-defeating way. For instance, thoughts such as 'I'm not going to pass for sure' may discourage you from working hard when you are preparing for your exams. The way you interpret events has a huge impact on the way how you feel and behave.

The Mechanism of Self-discussion

The relationship between your thoughts, feelings and behaviours can best be explained by the following:

- **The Situation:** This refers to the situation itself, or the things that happen when you start feeling bad, such as being at a party with a whole lot of people you don't know, being overloaded with your assignments, or making a silly comment that you later regret. When you identify this sort of situation which activates your internal discussion, it's important to stick to the facts, for example: 'I tried on my clothes and they were too tight', rather than 'I tried on my clothes and I looked so fat & ugly', or 'Tina smiled and said "hi" to me and I shied and looked away', rather than 'Tina smiled & said "hi" to me and I made a total idiot of myself'.

- **The Beliefs:** This comprises of our self-talk (thoughts) and assumptions that we make about a situation. Identifying our self-talk can sometimes be tricky. This is because it is so automatic that often we are not even aware of what is going on in our mind when something happens and we suddenly feel upset, we assume that it is the situation itself that is making of us feel this way. However it is not the situation but the way we perceive it (Our Beliefs) makes us feel the way we do. Our thoughts largely determine the way we feel, for example, your thoughts might be 'I've become really overweight...I must look so ugly... no wonder guys never talk to me'. Your feelings resulting from these thoughts might be sadness and frustration.
- **The Consequences**: The results of our belief include our feelings and behaviours. Feelings are emotions such as worry, anxiety, guilt, anger, embarrassment, joy, or excitement. Behaviours are the actions or things we do, such as communication, withdraw, ask for help, go for a jogging or stay in bed. Thinking negatively about situations makes you feel bad and it can also cause you to behave in an unhelpful way. In addition, negative self-talk leads you to low self-esteem. When you feel down it is likely that you are very hard on yourself, and that you will tend to criticize and judge yourself unfairly.

The worse you feel the more negative your self-talk is likely to become. We often blame ourselves when things go wrong, compare ourselves with others in a way that makes us feel inferior, exaggerate our weaknesses, focus on failures and predict that the worst will happen.

Let's Understand Through an Example

Here's an example to illustrate the process of self-talk:

Situation: You get your exam timetable.

Beliefs (Self-talk):

- "I'm not going to finish my course before exams"
- "I'll fail and the whole thing will be a disaster... My parents will be so disappointed with me"
- "I won't be able to get good results and then won't be able to build my career."

Results (Feelings and Behaviours):

- You feel stressed, panicky, butterflies in the stomach.
- You can't bring yourself to sit down and study.
- You sit down in front of the TV or Computer just killing your time.

What's the Solution?

The best way to understand the connection between Situation, Beliefs and the results is to see how it applies to your own situations. Why not have a go? Think of a situation in the last two weeks where you have found yourself feeling bad. For example, you may have been feeling upset, stressed, angry, sad, depressed, embarrassed or guilty. Briefly describe the situation in a 'stress-log', covering these three steps.

One of the most important skills for learning to deal with stressful situations is to identify your self-talk - the things you say to yourself inside your mind. The 'stress-log', covering the three steps of the situation is a useful tool to help you challenge the negative or unhelpful aspects of your thinking, and to replace them with more reasonable and helpful thoughts.

Famous Cyclist Lance Armstrong won "Tour de France" tournament many times before he was diagnosed with lung cancer. He was on the top of his career but suddenly everything was on the verge of vanishing. He kept on talking to himself in positive manner. He never thought of losing the battle with cancer. He took it as a normal disease. He kept on thinking that very soon he will be okay and is going to win yet another championship. Cycling was his passion, he never thought of living without it. It was the result of his positive self talk that he could heal that fatal disease. Later on he again participated in 'Tour de France' and emerged as champion yet another time.

How to Challenge Negative Discussions?

Even though you can't always control the situation you're in, you can change the way you think about it. The problem with self-talk is that it always feels true. Even though your thoughts might often be biased or incorrect, you tend to assume that they're facts when they're actually wrong or mistook perceptions. Self-talk is often directed towards the negative, and sometimes it's simply wrong. If you are experiencing depression, it is particularly likely that you interpret things negatively. That's why it's useful to keep an eye on the things you tell yourself, and challenge some of the negative aspects of your thinking. You can test, challenge and change your self-talk. You can change some of the negative aspects of your thinking by challenging the irrational parts and replacing them with more reasonable thoughts, the positive ones.

Challenging Your Self-Talk

Challenging your self-talk enables you to feel better and to respond to situations in a more helpful way. Learning to dispute negative thoughts might take time and practice, but is worth the effort! Once you start looking at it, you'll probably be surprised by how much of your thinking is inaccurate, exaggerated, or focused on the negativity of the situation. Whenever you find yourself feeling depressed, angry, anxious or upset, use this as your signal to stop and become aware of your thoughts.

A good way to test the accuracy of your perceptions might be to ask yourself some challenging question. These questions will help you to check out your self-talk to see whether your current view is reasonable. This will also help you discover other ways of thinking about your situation.

When you feel anxious, depressed or stressed-out your self-talk is likely to become extreme - you'll be more likely to expect the worst and focus on the most negative aspects of your situation. So, it's helpful to try and put things into their proper perspective.

Have Focused Approach

Is thinking this way helping me to feel good or to achieve my goals?

- What can I do to help myself solve the problem?

- Is there something I can learn from this situation, to help me do it better next time?

Recognizing that your current way of thinking might be self-defeating (i.e. it doesn't make you feel good or help you to get what you want) can sometimes motivate you to look at things from a different perspective.

Don't say negative for what you want to achieve: A friend of mine aspired to be a Chartered Accountant. But he always said that a fool like me can never be a CA. This implies his thinking process and his words went against his own efforts. By our words and thoughts we can either empower our actions or weaken them. Our words and our thoughts should be in consonance with our actions and aspirations only then we can turn our dreams to reality.

Changing the way you think about things may not be easy at first, but with time and practice, you will get better. Give it a go - it's worth the effort!

Common Mistakes

In addition to the negative or unhelpful thinking described in the 'Challenging Negative Thinking' fact sheet, there are some common thinking errors that most of us make from time to time. Thinking errors are irrational patterns of thinking that cause you to feel bad, and sometimes to act in self-defeating ways. Whenever you find yourself feeling upset (e.g. anxious, angry, depressed, resentful, guilty, ashamed, etc) look for any thinking errors that might be contributing to the way you felt.

Challenging Your Wrong Thinking

Here are 10 common thinking errors and ways to challenge them.

1. **Good and Bad Thinking**

   When you're thinking good and bad, you see everything in terms of being good or bad. Either you are great or you are a loser. If you don't look like a model you must be ugly. If you do something wrong, then you are completely bad. You see everything as either good or bad, with no in-between.

   Look for In between situation: It is important to avoid thinking about things in terms of extremes. Most things aren't good and bad – usually they are somewhere in-between. Just because something isn't completely perfect doesn't mean that it's a complete write-off.

Ask yourself:

- Is it really so bad, or am I seeing things in good and bad?
- How else can I think about the situation?
- Am I taking an extreme view?

2. **Unfair Comparisons**

   Another common thinking error is making unfair comparisons between certain individuals and yourself. When you do this, you compare yourself with people who have a specific advantage in some area. Making unfair comparisons can leave you feeling inadequate and not OK.

Stop Making Unfair Comparisons

Ask yourself:

- Am I comparing myself with people who have a particular advantage?
- Am I making fair comparisons?

3. **Negative Filtering**

   When you filter you do two things: First you hone in on the negative aspects of your situation and secondly, you ignore or dismiss all the positive aspects.

Consider the Whole Picture

Ask yourself:

- Am I looking at the negatives, while ignoring the positives?
- Is there a more balanced way to look at this?

4. **The Self-Blame Game**

   When you personalize, you feel responsible for anything that goes wrong, even when it's not your fault or responsibility.

Don't Personalize

It's important to consider that not everything is your fault or your responsibility. Most things have more than one cause.

Ask yourself:

- Am I really to blame? Is this all about me?
- What other explanations might there be for this situation?

5. **What People Think?**

   We often think we know what other people are thinking. We assume that others are focused on our faults and weaknesses - but this is often wrong!

Don't assume that you know what others are thinking.

Ask yourself:

- What is the evidence? How do I know what other people are thinking?

- Just because I assume something, does that mean I'm right?

6. Exaggeration

You generally exaggerate the consequences when things go wrong, and you imagine that things are or will be disastrous.

Don't Exaggerate:

Ask Yourself:

- What's the worst thing that can happen?
- What's the best thing that can happen?
- What's the most likely to happen?
- Is there anything good about the situation?
- Is there any way to fix the situation?

7. Labelling

When you use labelling you might call yourself (or other people) names. Instead of being specific (e.g. 'that was a silly thing to say') you make negative generalizations about yourself or other people (e.g. 'I am weak', 'I am dumb', 'I'm a loser', I'm boring'; 'She is an idiot').

Stick to the Facts:

Ask yourself:

- What are the facts and what are my interpretations?
- Just because there is something that I'm not happy with, does that mean that I'm totally no good?

The Effect of Challenging Thinking Errors

What is the effect of challenging your thinking errors? Does it make you feel better? Does it encourage you to change some of your behaviour? Often it is useful to write down the changes that occur after you have challenged your thinking, as this helps you to see the advantages of working on your thoughts, and motivates you to keep doing so. REMEMBER!! Whenever you are Feeling Bad, Try to Become Aware of Your Thoughts. If they are negative or critical, have a go at challenging them. Once you get into the habit of disputing your negative self-talk you'll find it easier to handle difficult situations, and as a result, you'll feel less stressed and more confident and in control.

Write it Down

While you are learning to identify and challenge your negative self-talk it's a good idea to write it all down. Writing down your thoughts and disputing statements in a diary or notebook helps you to develop your skills. Initially it might feel like work, but the more often you do it, the easier it will become, and the better you will feel.

Try it Out

Now that you know a few common thinking errors and how to challenge them, why don't you try it out? It might not be easy at first, and it may take some time. However, the rewards could be huge! People who choose the way they think about things, who are at peace with the past, live in the present, and are optimistic about the future, are generally happier.

3

Dreams, The Blue Print

Once God whispered to a baby, before sending him to this world,

My Child!!! You are dearest to me.

There was an era

When I dreamt about a complete space to accompany me,

To culminate my solitude,

And then,

I realized my dream.

I made you and this whole universe.

My child! You are so dear to me.

I have conferred the most crucial and mystic vigour of mine, of watching dreams, to you.

My child! You are my dream and you are so valued by me.

I have also given to you the mightiest of my powers,

The power of realizing one's own dreams

Yes my child! I have given that to you only.

Enjoy dear! ***None of my creations but you can conceive dreams.***

And none but you can work to realize them.

Yes you! You my child! **Only you***!*

You are so dear to me.

Enjoy dear! ***Use these powers to get what you wish for and live the life you dream of. Go my child, enjoy!"***

Dreams are Precious

Going through the above fraction, we come to realize the significance of dreams, which in fact, are blessings of the almighty to all of us.

Dreaming, sensibly, is considered as a reckless/ improvident activity by most of the practical personnel of today's world. For them, life is 'now & here'. To handle the situations at hand is their object. But, how to handle the situations in the best possible manner and how to be proactive enough to alter the situations which approach you before they come, is what dreams tell us. Please consider! The dreams, which are talked about here, are not the ones, which are seen whilst sleeping, but the ones, which we witness through open eyes.

And somebody has rightly quoted "Those are not dreams which we see while sleeping but dreams are those which never let us sleep."

We all are aware to the fact that dreams do act as stress-busters for us even when we are in utter anxiety. But that is not only why they are bestowed to us. Yes, dreams are endowed to us by our father, the father of all, the almighty, not only to imagine the life we want, but also to make it true. All what we require is to put faith in our own dreams.

"Never let yesterday's disappointments overshadow tomorrow's dreams."

Yes, why don't you own dreams as if they are your own property, why don't you recognize that dreaming is also one of your birthrights and why don't you dare enough to utilize them to live the life you love. Why don't you use them to increase your worthiness by just deciding once that you have to make it true? Now most of you will wonder if dreams can be used to enhance our worthiness. Yes, but you know what- *'FREE HAS NO VALUE'. We all don't care for this precious gift of God to us and blame these innocent dreams for our failures. In fact, each and every one of us should treasure dreams for we are very lucky to have them.*

Don't let anyone steal your dream.
It's your dream, not theirs.
- Dan Zadra

Again do consider, I am talking about the kind of dreams concerning what you want to accomplish and be in your life, and those, which you watch with your eyes wide-open.

For instance, let's imagine a student, poor in mathematics, who is always scolded in the classroom. Whenever he sits at home to do his homework, he gets reminded of the words of his teacher, "You can't do anything right. You will never get it. You are a duffer..." These words have made a home inside him and the results take the form of a vicious circle. Now he can't even think of performing in that subject. All he used to do is to dream that if he would also be a kind of student dear to his teacher, how happy he would be. Now what is the remedy? ....

........Yes!! That's it. His dream! **That's just where it starts, with a dream.** Somebody like **me** approaches him,,,,, (ha ha...let me enjoy the dream) convinces him to forget his collapse, gives him the dream to outperform in mathematics, makes him imagine and believe **that he is already a success in mathematics and stick to this fact enough to correspond according to it.** Now please stop! Please do read it again. Just think over it. What does it mean? Is he going to behave in a self-important manner in front of his teacher the next day… or something like that?……Answer is - No………to behave and '**correspond according to his dream**' means something else. Please, for a minute, just step into the shoes of a student who is very dear to the teacher. Dear friend! Even he has to perform very well to manage his part of image in front of his teacher. He has to learn each and every lesson of the teacher by heart, more than any other student is expected to. But the difference is he does his job happily and without any stress. So the student, who has stepped into the shoes of an intelligent student, makes a new **beginning** by forgetting all what he had experienced in past and that too, happily. Yet he does not behave as freely in the classroom as the intelligent one but at least he behaves in a self-respective manner. More than anything else, now he daily watches new dreams relating to his mathematics class and his performance, and works harder and even harder to realize them. He's happy to work to watch his dream coming true. He is able to do this because he believes in a newer facet of himself. And you know what, one-day, very soon, he will come to recognize that he actually embodied his dream all along and he just had not realized it.

So?

So, at least now, we can believe in the power of dreams…well, if dreams can work in the case of a below-average student, then why won't the same work in our case?

Remember!!!

All we need is to trust and value it.

Dreams: Way to Happiness

Once, a person was having a lot of problems. Whatever he tried ended with failures. He was feeling very down. On advice of one of his friends, he met a Saint and asked him the way to get a hold of happiness. The Saint told him to have DREAMS. Hearing this he got annoyed and told Saint not to tease him. He further asked him, "Sir, I am facing problems and troubles, I came to you to know the way to happiness. Instead of giving a solution, you are asking me to dream! Are you serious?"

Saint asked him when he would get Happiness.

He replied that whenever he gets success in his endeavours, he would be happy,

Saint asked him when he would get success.

He replied that when his actions are correct, it would result in Success.

Saint further asked him when he would do Actions.

He replied that when he has plans.

Saint asked him when he would have Plans.

He replied that when he sets his goals.

Saint asked him when he would set Goals.

He replied that when he identifies needs.

Saint asked him how he would identify Needs.

He replied that he would identify from his wants.

Finally saint asked him when he would get wants.

He replied that when he DREAMS.

Yes, *DREAMS will generate your WANTS*

WANTS will identify your NEEDS

NEEDS will set your GOALS

GOALS will push you to PLAN

PLANS will result in ACTIONS

ACTIONS will end with SUCCESS

SUCCESS will make you HAPPY

"WAKE UP TO THE POWER OF DREAMS"

Your dreams spark off an uncontrollable urge in you to achieve and outperform. The events you participate and experience, if excellent, triggers off a want in you to repeat or outclass the present. The dreams are the stepping-stones to those distant achievements and honours. Without dreams you will not be able to start off.

In fact,

To have a dream is the same as being successful right away!

Believe In Your Dreams

The only thing required is that we have to believe in our dreams and the power attached with them.

Future belongs to those who believe in their dreams.

- Eleanor Roosevelt

If determined, dreams could very well be used: - as a problem solving tool.

- To function more effectively during waking hours.
- To enhance and deepen creativity.
- To help focus career goals and true purpose in life.

- To provide insights into health problems.
- To help bring balance to one's life.

All you need is to just visualize the change you want to bring in your life **as if it is well within your reach** and you can successfully achieve it.

Changing the State

Step #1: Identify the behavior you want to change. Now make an internal representation of that behavior as you see it through your own eyes. If you want to stop biting your fingernails, imagine a picture of you lifting your hand, bringing your fingers to your lips and biting your nails.

Step#2: Once you have a clear picture of the behaviour you want to change or a position you want to attain, you need to create a different representation, a picture of yourself as you would be if you made the desired change and what that change would mean to you. You might picture yourself taking your fingers away from your mouth, creating a little pressure on the finger you were going to bite and seeing your nails perfectly manicured and yourself as well dressed, magnificently groomed, more in control and more confident. The picture you make of yourself in that we want to create an ideal internal representation, one that you will continue to be drawn to rather than one you feel you already have.

Dare to Dream

Dream, dream, dream; it costs nothing.
When you cease to dream you cease to live.

- Malcolm Forbes

As we grow up, all of us have dreams about what we would like to do. The happiest people seem to be the ones living out their dreams in some way as adults.

But most of us don't live the life of our dreams. It is because some people lose sight of their dreams; others may see their dreams die; still others have forgotten what their dreams once were.

Whatever the reasons for not living out your dreams, my work with people has taught me to be enough of an optimist to believe we can dream again.

If you find yourself unable to live your dream, what happened?

While it's all well and good to dream, for dreams to become real we have to take action toward the dream.

Richard Bach says,

"You are never given a wish without the power to make it come true. You may have to work for it, however."

Power of Your Subconscious

Let me share something important with you...

Can you remember a time when you were driving somewhere, you finally arrived at your destination, and you have no idea how you got there?

Think about that for a minute - you turned corners, stopped at intersections, didn't hit any pedestrians, and used your indicators, your brake, your accelerator... maybe you even changed gears. **And you can't recall any of it...**

Your subconscious mind took control and drove the car while your conscious mind focused on something else.

Well believe it or not, that's **exactly how it happens in life...** Your subconscious mind has control. And, it's driving you to the life destination that it believes you want to go too!

Your actions and behaviors *without even realizing it*, follow your subconscious instructions. Just like your body followed its instructions when you were driving the car...

"Take this turn, stop at this juncture" etc all without *"consciously and intentionally"* thinking about it.

As you awaken to the idea that your subconscious is taking you on a journey, you also begin to realize the possibility that **the journey and the final destination may not be where you want to go!**

It's Time For You To Know The Truth!

With this new awakening you can begin to understand that ***where you are now - is Not your fault***.

It's years of programming, that builds your **deeply ingrained subconscious program**. Or more appropriately: the core values and beliefs that govern your life.

Your core values and beliefs control what you think about, the people you identify with, the way in which you handle money, your level of self-expression, the people you choose as friends and companions...and the goals in which you aspire to.

Most of us adapted these long ago from our parents, teachers, friends or media... and, although they may mean well, often the messages and beliefs they instill in young people are fear-based and limiting. ***They're also very difficult to erase.***

Thus, our minds tend to become too "over-crowded" with negative thoughts and chatter, deeply ingrained bad habits, and old programs that keep sabotaging our effort to bring *positive change* into our lives...

So subtle is this process that you may go through your entire life burdened by it, never recognizing its presence.

But now, it's time to...UNLEASH the True Hidden Genius inside you and claim the things you want from life.

Imagine for a moment, what it feels like, if you have *everything* in your life you truly desire? *A deep love with your partner... an endless supply of cash... success and recognition... a totally fulfilling life and more, much more...*

Well, the good news is.

You DO Have The Power To Rewrite Your Reality...

(And, it's actually easier than you think!)...

A number of methods have been created over the years to **change your subconscious programming**. Affirmations are just one example. Now don't get me wrong, affirmations can, and do, change your subconscious.

BUT it's got to be unfailingly consistent! You have to do or play "battle" with your conscious mind to allow your **new beliefs of success and happiness** into your subconscious (the REAL powerhouse). *So...*

"Believe in yourself and in your dream,
Though impossible things may seem
Someday, somehow you'll get through
To the goal you have in view.
Mountains fall and seas divide,
Before the one who in his stride
Takes a hard road by day

Sweeping obstacles away
Believe in yourself and in your plan
Say not - I cannot - I can
The prizes of life we fail to win
Because we doubt the power within..."

- Anonymous

YOU'RE POWER!
IS AS OLD AS TIME ITSELF

This *endless potential (your subconscious),* which lives inside you... has been around since time began. It's only now we are beginning to rediscover it - and to get a glimmering insight into its *wonderful power.*

Your ancient ancestors **uncovered certain truths** - which even today, with all our education and technology, we have somehow managed to overlook, or have simply forgotten about...

Even the spiritual and religious communities have made reference of this power. *The Bible* and nearly all-Eastern philosophies have spoken about this principle for many thousands of years:

Jesus the **Buddha** and even people like **Gandhi** have used this "Secret Power" (the subconscious) to create miracles...

"Look at what I can do. And know that these things, and more, shall you also do. For have I not said, ye are Gods?"

- Jesus

"We are what we think. All that we are arises with our thoughts. And with our thoughts, we make our world"

- Buddha

"Happiness is when what you think, what you say, and what you do are in harmony"

- Gandhi

Now... don't you think, it's time you get in touch with the real YOU! - And reclaim back you're long lost *power* and *endless potential?*

How Can You Do This?

Just as surely as a magnet draws to itself every piece of iron, which comes within its reach, there is nothing of good you can ask for, which this power cannot bring you!

Your mind is a very powerful and amazing tool, which is literally packed with endless potential – and is easily capable of attaining levels of power, consciousness and performance far beyond what many people imagine possible...so dear! Use it! Use it to dream, to think that you can, to believe that you can, to design your life, at least in your mind. Remember! With your dreams is attached your heart and the project which will encompass your heart will surely be able to infuse in you the enthusiasm to work for it.

Your work is to discover your world and then with all your heart give yourself to it.

- Buddha

You have brains in your head.
You have feet in your shoes.
You can steer yourself in any direction you choose.
You're on your own.
And you know what you know.
You are the guy who'll decide where to go.

- Dr. Seuss

Practicing for 21 days

Further I want to say is dreams have got the power not only to increase the heights of your achievements but also can they enhance the quality of your daily life, to cultivate new thought process, to change habits. All you need is to put a consistent effort. In the initial phase when you start thinking different from what you have been thinking, your conscious mind will reject it. But to make it believe you need to think it regularly, and may be for two or three weeks, say about 21 days.

Remember:

Once Subconscious accepts an idea it starts executing the same. Therefore, you can give any damn idea to it.

Do you have these words in your vocabulary: "You can't, you will fail, you have not got a chance, you are all wrong, you are weak, you are too old you can't win/excel and things are getting worse".

Now you have to think in contrast.

Think good and good follows. Think evil and evil follows. You are what you think all day long.

Think & visualize in sleepy or drowsy state in the late night just before sleeping or early in the morning just before getting up from the bed. Your subconscious is most receptive in the drowsy state. Therefore, this is the best time to send inputs to your subconscious.

If you want to leave some bad habit of yours, you visualize that you have left it. If you are poor in maths, you visualize that you are doing superb in that subject; you are helping others and scoring brilliant marks in the examination.

Subconscious is the ultimate tool to attain what you dream because 90% of your mental life is subconscious.

To cultivate confidence, learn to trust yourself. Listen to your inner voice (Subconscious), your gut and try to erase the ghosts of self-doubts. Remember also, that you have control over how you choose to see situations. You decide whether or not self-doubt will hold you back. When you go after your dreams and put things in the right perspective, your confidence will soar, as will your ability to succeed.

I somewhere read an interesting drama seen which is played in China. The play goes in this fashion:

A person dies and goes to heaven.

He enters the first gate and confronts huge and luxurious houses, and then he enters the next gate and witness abundant jewellery and ornaments.

He further enters another gate and notices many more luxuries lying idle.

After observing all these he questions God. "Why you have kept all these things here? If they are of no use, why don't you give them to your followers who are living miserably on the earth?".

Then god replies in a cool way

"My son these things have absolutely been kept for those people only, but they don't make enough endeavours to get them".

This story fits on each one of you. You have all skills, talents and opportunities but you never realize them and end with nothing. At the day end you blame your destiny.

It's time to realize the importance of hidden treasure within you. You need to believe it.

Think & Get

"As you sow, so shall you reap". You can't expect mangoes from a babul tree. You have seen the miraculous powers of your subconscious. Now it's on you in which direction you want to proceed. But I can assure you if you are heading in a right direction, you are guiding your subconscious in right manner, and you will attain your dreams.

When I was reading few books on the power of thinking and power of subconscious mind, I thought of experimenting it on someone. I was on a visit to my friends place and noticed an adolescent guy who was stranger to me. I asked my friend about him and he told that he is distant cousin and came from village for further studies. When that boy served water to me I asked him, what are you doing?, he said "Sir I have just passed my 10th Standard exam and wish to go for next standard with Science biology." My next question was, Why? He was prompt enough to reply, "Because I want to become a doctor." After enquiring further I came to know that he was a mediocre student with 53% marks scored in Xth standard. It was almost impossible for him to get admission in science with that percentage but due to influence of my friend he could get admission in an ordinary school. In spite of what he had scored I was impressed with the clear aspiration the boy had. I immediately suggested him a course of action to be followed if he wants to achieve his dreams. I asked him to bring a note book and instructed him to write few sentences. The first sentence I asked him to write 1. "For the last time in my life I used recommendation to get admission." 2. In XIth standard I will score more than 70% marks, 3. In XIIth standard I will score more than 75% marks, 4. In the first attempt I will qualify medical entrance exam, 5. I will keep my rank high so that I can get admission in a reputed medical college. Like this I dictated him to write 10 sentences relating to his future projections and instructed him to write them every day in the morning followed by reading in the night before going to sleep. After couple of month when I was again at my friends place I remembered that I gave an assignment to that young chap. When I saw him I asked him to get that note book, he followed my instruction and in less than 10 seconds time he was in front of me with that note book. I was literally stunned seeing the note book. The boy did his assignment without any deviation. That day I realized the boy is going to make it. Let me quote for you all, that boy scored 72% in XIth standard, 76% in twelfth standard and got admitted to one of the premier coaching institute for medical entrance exam preparation. In the very first attempt he qualified the medical entrance exam with reasonably good rank. Recently he finished his MBBS from a reputed college of India. How could he make it? Why many students having better educational background and better scores in the previous exams could not do it? Answer is very clear. Through that process of writing and reading the series of aspirations or dreams on daily basis he could inculcate them into his subconscious mind and that made the whole difference.

After successful experimentation of the concept I applied it on myself and till date I have attained half a dozen things which I dreamt five years back, looks unbelievable but it's sure shot process to proceed towards the desired destination.

My Experiments with Dreams

I have few instances to share which are very relevant in this context. I was participant in a four days residential work shop "VEDA" at Goa in July 2001. During one session we were asked to write down specific goals in different areas which we wanted to achieve in next 5 years. Before writing I gave it a thought, should I write realistic figures or something big. I opted to write something big and exceptional. I myself had a sarcastic smile on my face while writing those goals. What I wrote was that I want my personal and bigger house, a new car, a foreign trip and a monthly income which was almost 5 times of my current income.

On the day of valedictory we were given a certificate for the participation along with a small booklet which contained the goals of next 5 years written by me during the workshop. When I was on the way back to my place I kept on staring at those goals. After reaching back I kept that booklet close to my bed and used to read that.

Now what happened after that?

I had my first foreign trip only after 20 days of the workshop.

I was in my new house in May 2004.

I got an opportunity to work as service providing company to GE Countrywide in February 2002 and my income reached to the level what I mentioned in my goals.

I bought new car in 2003.

And you know I was not aware that this has happened to me. Actually when I was rearranging my library books in October 2004 and suddenly that workshop booklet came in my hands. I curiously opened that goal page and started reading that. Only this came out of my mouth "Oh my god" those big goals which were apparently looking impossible to be achieved in 5 years are almost achieved in 3.5 years time.

It was not less than a miracle for me and I started believing in power of dreaming.

I started imparting soft skills and behavioural training from the year 2000 but never thought or aspired to conduct seminars overseas. In 2005 when I was returning back from Jaipur from an official assignment and had a small dream during a nap in the train. What I saw that I was standing in front of so many foreigners and delivering my seminar in a fluent style. After couple of minutes when I was in conscious state I gave it a thought and made it a point that I am going to visualize about this until it happens in real.

I started dreaming about conducting seminar abroad but had no clue how it is going to be executed. In June 2006 I was going to Singapore & Malaysia for family vacation and somehow one day prior to my departure I came to know about my friend's brother working in a software company in Singapore. After knowing about my profile he himself proposed for a seminar for his company's employees during my visit. I was thrilled and extremely happy. Yet another dream of mine was coming true.

In the year 2008 I got yet another opportunity to conduct a seminar in Busan (South Korea) in the Asia Pacific Conference of Junior chamber International. It was a super hit and appreciated by all the participants. Since then I have travelled to Europe, Africa, Middle East and all most all major Asian countries to conduct my seminars. People from more than 50 countries have attended my seminars conducted in different international conventions.

I have shared few important glimpses of my experiments with dreams. I have 'N' number of instances where I perceived or visualized a situation and I found it to be real later on.

If you want to attain what you aspire, don't let your aspirations die till the time you attain it. Keep the dreams under your visibility, keep your daily schedule like that you remember, read or see what you are going to achieve.

"What your mind conceives and heart believes you can achieve it."

- Napoleon Hill

Do you believe in yourself as much as you could? Do you believe enough in yourself that can make you believe your dreams? Being confident makes all the difference when it comes to beg decisions in your life. When you have a sure feeling about yourself, you are less likely to go back and forth; uncertain of the actions you should take. Be strong in your convictions.

Your subconscious mind accepts what is impressed upon it or what you consciously believe. It does not reason things out as your conscious mind does, and it does not argue with you controversially. Your subconscious mind is like **a bed of soil that accepts any kind of seeds.** If you sow seeds of wheat the soil will grow the same and if you sow weeds it will grow the same. Negative, destructive thoughts continue to work negatively in your subconscious mind. Sooner or later, they will emerge and take shape as an outer experience that corresponds to their content.

So we say you to imagine the life you want to live, to believe that you can get it and finally to get it.

When we visit to zoo, we usually see an elephant tied with a pole by a thin chain. Don't you think that the elephant can't break it? Certainly he can. But he thinks he can't so he doesn't try. Not easy to believe but understand the process why he doesn't try. When elephant was a baby elephant and was brought to zoo from jungle was tied with a thick chain which was very difficult for him to break. The baby elephant tried so many times but could not break it and every time he failed a thought was conceived that this is too thick to break or I am not strong enough to get away with this. After this thought becomes permanent and transmitted to conscious mind, the conscious stops working on it. After a month or so the baby elephant stops trying as he knows he can't break the chain. After a year the baby elephant has become a giant one and still not trying to break it, despite all the physical capabilities he is not trying because there is a permanent thought stored inside that he can't break it. We also form such limitations and thoughts after some negative experiences in our life and learn to live with them. You never try to break shackles, before you try start changing what you have stored in your subconscious as well.

You can strategically inculcate what you want to, it may be related to learning a new skill or leaving a bad habit. Before you set any goal you set it in your subconscious.

The working-at-it involves setting goals for you. Setting goals to work toward your dreams is simply *breaking your large dream down into manageable pieces.*

A wise person once said, "*A goal is-simply a dream with a deadline.*"

Therefore, ***the only thing, which takes its place before planning to achieve goals and even before goal setting, is nothing but the DREAM***

You have to expect things of yourself before you can do them.

- Michael Jordan

Dreams are today's answers to tomorrow's questions.

- Edgar Cayce

Here are some questions for you:

Are you living out any of your dreams?

If yes, consider what it took and what you did to get there. If no, what got in the way?

Is it possible to resurrect any of the old dreams?

If you were to dream again, what would it be about?

Always believe the fact,

Whatever your biggest desire or dream is right now; YOU HAVE THE ABILITY to realize it.

It's truly within your reach...

It makes no difference **how desperate** your situation is ... or **how out of reach** your dreams may seem to you today... you can *finally break free from the restraints of your current life and finally you can realize your dreams...*

If one dream should fall and break into a thousand pieces, never be afraid to pick one of those pieces up and begin again.

- Flavia

Remember,

To have a dream is the same as being successful right away!

Dream High

Dreams are free, so free your dreams.

- Astrid Alauda

Dream is not something, which you watch when you sleep;
Dream is something, which doesn't let you sleep.

- Dr. A.P.J.Abdul Kalam

Years after Disneyland was built, after the completion of Walt Disney World, the story goes that someone went up to Mike Vance, the Creative Director for Walt Disney Studios and said, "Isn't it too bad Walt Disney didn't live to see this?"

Without pausing, he replied,

"BUT HE DID SEE IT, THAT'S WHY IT'S HERE."

"Do not think that what is hard for thee to master is impossible for man; but if a thing is possible and proper for man, deem it attainable by thee."

- Marcus Aurelius

The height of wisdom is to dream high enough not to lose the dream in the seeking of it.

-William Faulkner

Keep away from people who try to belittle your ambitions. Small people always do that, but the really great make you feel that you, too, can become great.

- Mark Twain

4

Attitude, The Decisive Factor

The greatest discovery of our generation is that human beings can alter their lives by altering their attitudes of mind. As you think, so shall you be.

- William James

Lots of discussion, researches, studies and surveys have taken place in the world to find out the secret of success. In this process many conclusions were reached upon, many secrets were revealed. A group of people contributed that we need money to be successful in life but after lot of deliberations on that finding, it was proved not to be the secret. There were numerous examples where people didn't have money but they became successful and rocked. Another group of people believed that if you have good education, it paves the way to success. But it was found that having good education doesn't ensure success for you. If it was so, then every Harvard, oxford or IIM graduate would have been in the list of successful people of the world. Finally after lots of researches it was concluded that positive attitude is the most critical factor which contributes maximally in somebody's success. The irony is, most people are ignorant about this fact and in spite of having all other attributes except positive mental attitude they struggle in life and don't reach at place where they ought to have reached.

Talent Alone can't Produce the Desired Results

I have seen many people around me with immense amount of talent and I used to wonder why they could not reach on top and struggled with mediocrity all throughout their life. And then I realized after watching their life closely that they were not having the right attitude. Talent alone doesn't give you winning edge unless you have winning and positive attitude to make things happen in right direction. Bad attitude coupled with no talent makes you worst person, Bad attitude coupled with Good talent makes you a bad person, Good attitude coupled with average talent or average attitude coupled with good talent makes you a good person. But Good attitude coupled with good talent certainly makes you a great personality.

What is ATTITUDE?

Webster's New Collegiate Dictionary says attitude is "a mental position with regard to a fact or state". Our "mental position" is something we can manage and control, if we opt to. Means – attitude is the way we choose to view the world. It is a matter of outlook & is definitely a matter of choice. We alone are responsible for cultivating the attitude that brings us the results we want and deserve. Therefore, in other words, attitude is the filter through which all the thoughts, pros and cons relating to any situation are filtered. And we are to decide which thoughts shall pass out through the filter and which shall remain as filtrate. We can evaluate and weigh the facts, draw our conclusions and choose our attitude instead of letting things and people outside control our mental position.

Your attitude can be best friend or worst enemy of yours. The attitude keeps all past records in its storage and speaks those experiences in present and accordingly defines our future. Good attitude may not guarantee you the success but negative or bad attitude surely determines your failure.

You all have two situations or alternatives. You can compile a list of "positive responses" and another list of "negative reactions". The list may look like this:

Negative reactions	Positive responses
Oh, I am running short of time and have no time for myself.	I have busy schedule but I can find time for activities let me plan and balance it properly.
My relationships going sour with many people day by day and I am helpless!	I need to control my behaviour and reaction. I believe in good relationship and I can nurture and maintain good relationships.
My financial position is getting tight day by day. I have scarcity of money and I am helpless.	I know I am running little short of money. Still I can manage my finances. Let me plan it a fresh and cut budget of unnecessary things. I can control my finances.
Oh, I am getting old! Oh woe is me!	Praise the God, I am getting old! There is only one alternative to getting old and I'd rather live!

This list is endless. Now, when someone comes up to you and asks, "How are you?" you are required to make a choice about which list you are going to tell them about! You can tell them about your good responses or your negative reactions. It's up to you, how do u respond. You know many time people ask us the same question

"How are you?" and many of us reply "Just okay" and very few say "Fantastic", it just reflects your attitude.

You cannot choose what will happen to you. You cannot guarantee success and happiness for yourself. These things are out of your control. However, you can choose how to feel about these things, about how to respond to such situations.

Right Attitude – Key to Happiness

There once were two brothers. One boy was an optimist and the other was a pessimist. You couldn't knock the optimist's attitude down. He rolled with the punches, smiled and found the good in any situation. But, it was difficult to ever bring sunshine into the life of the pessimist. He always found something to be unhappy about! One day their father did an experiment with the two boys. He took the pessimist into a room filled with video games, toys, bicycles, candies, and a big screen TV. The father told the pessimist that he could play with everything in the room. The father took the optimist to another room filled with horse manure and told him he could play with everything in the room. Later he checked on both boys. The pessimist was finding something critical to say about everything available to him. The toys were not the right ones, the video games would probably be too easy, his friend at school had a bigger TV and the candy was sure to spoil before he could get it eaten. The father went to the other room and found his other son gleefully digging into the pile of manure. He looked up and excitedly exclaimed, "With all this manure, there's got to be a pony in here somewhere!"

The important thing to note is this: "which boy was happier? And why?" It matters less what your circumstances are in life or what you have! What matters far more is how you choose to evaluate and react to your circumstances in life. You could be happy in nearly any circumstances if you got our attitude right!

There's another story - USE-LESS!

A robust man called up the police to complain about a robbery at his house. The thieves were a couple of thin and rather weak men armed with only a small knife. The constable was amazed to write down a seemingly unending list of valuables burgled............... In exasperation he asked, "Did they leave any valuable behind?" The complainant promptly replied, "my pistol worth Rs 80,000/-"

The cop was curious, "How did they miss the gun?" The beaming complainant said, "I was sitting on it." The shocked officer asked, "Why didn't you use it to stop the thieves?" The man sheepishly replied, "Oh, it never occurred to me? I was too worried that they might see it and steal it because of its expensive worth..."

It is pertinent to note that a thing intended for his protection was useless because it was not used. His "using" the gun and using it would have saved valuables. We may laugh, but it is true that we could well be like the man who did not use what he had! For instance, our ability to smile can tackle a difficult situation. Nevertheless, it is in a difficulty that the smile is not used!

We possess knowledge and skills, a brain and a heart, our senses and our emotions. We have abilities. We have potential. There is so much that we possess. However, if we do not use the things we have, then the most valuable of our qualities and our strengths are of no use. More importantly, it is not enough to only "use" but also to use "enough". I believe that if you "use less" than our strengths are rendered "useless"! Without appropriate action, every possession is useless!

Therefore, one should accept oneself with all the flaws within one and one should accept all the possessions with one with complete grace and express gratitude to god for all what he has given to one and be happy, instead of grieving for what one is not having, and then, one should make efforts to avail the maximum happiness out of one's own possessions by utilizing the most of them.

Knowing Your Skills & Potentials, which are Invisible Like Air in the Glass

A glass half filled by water may seem to be half empty. The same glass can be viewed in a different perspective. A glass half filled by water is also half filled by air. And hence the glass is completely filled. Similarly in our life we all our bestowed with unique qualities and talents by God. But we see our lives like the half empty portion of the glass just because we fail to discover them in us. A positive approach to life will help us trace out those elements in our personality that may help us outshine in the world. A positive mindset helps us complete our life and make it more worth living.

Always remember – "Success is not the key to happiness but it is the happiness that leads to success".

And the key to happiness is nothing but right attitude.

Well Friends!!! Nonetheless, it is not so that you can just think positive about something and it will change. No, positive thinking does not change things. It does change YOU and the way you see things which actually helps in going through with it easily.

Does that mean you should accept any hand you have been dealt and not try to change it?

Absolutely not!

One should believe in the prayer: "Lord grant me the serenity to accept the things I can't change, the courage to change what I can, and the wisdom to know the difference." Many of us need the most help with the "wisdom to know the difference." We often try to change things that can't be changed, while accepting other things that can be changed, if we just try once!

Practice makes a man perfect:

Maintaining a positive attitude requires a conscious effort and discipline. Attitude control is based on the principle – Practice makes a man perfect. We are going to mess up sometimes, but we can practice and get better and better at it!

IS SOMETHING WRITTEN IN YOUR HOROSCOPE THAT YOU CAN'T DO THAT…

Ask People How many are suffering from self confidence problem. 80% will say yes, then, I ask how did they come to know about it? Was it diagnosed by a doctor or is it written in their Horoscope? The answer is simply no. Then how did they identify this disease? Yes, self confidence problem is a disease. Because it's not a fact and it's just a psychological assumption, that is why I call it a disease. May be the first time they went on the stage or the first time they tried a new thing they were scared, they could not perform well. But this is something normal. Anything that is new or unknown is always accompanied by such feelings and physical indications due to the uncertainty associated with it. The more we practice that thing, the more we gain knowledge about it, the more we get expertise in it, the lesser is that fear factor and gradually our confidence level enhances. Thus that tough iceberg of self confidence illusion can be shattered down by the solid attack of consistent practice.

Nothing is Impossible

Attitude doesn't just affect the way we feel. It also affects our reality!

Have you ever worked around a "no-sayer", a person who reacts to most ideas with an "it can't be done" attitude? We have all probably run into that type before. Do you think you will see a "no-sayer" invent a light bulb, or find a cure for cancer, or design a machine that will fly or discover a new country or a new source of energy? I don't think so. Do you think the Wright brothers, or Thomas Edison, or Columbus were "it can't be done" kind of people? I don't think so. The "no-sayer" with the "it can't be done" attitude is absolutely right in perception about himself because he will never do the things to make the "impossible" happen. He will actually work to justify why "it can't be done" and anyhow sabotage the success. Am I right?

Remember -

"A task is impossible if the doer believes it can't be done. The same task is possible if its doer believes he/she can do it. Therefore, impossible is merely a state of mind that prevents great things from happening!"

Impossible is an attitude ("a mental position with regard to a fact or state"). That's all it is. If we let this attitude set up house in our minds, it will form an immense barrier between us and the possibility of some great or better thing happening in our lives. Remember -

'Nothing is impossible'! Even the word 'impossible' says 'I m possible'.

Negative Attitude is More Contagious

Negative attitude spreads faster than positive one. Many people think that conceiving a negative thought does not make any difference, sometime they think that reacting negatively will make them stand differently. But they forget to note that while conceiving a negative thought they put extra lot of garbage in their mind and unintentionally the mind is becoming a dustbin. If you are having negative mindset, it spreads very fast and very soon the others in the environment start, getting affected, whereas, it takes more efforts to spread the positive attitude in the environment. Therefore be careful and keep yourself away from negative thoughts.

Once a man was passing through a bridge and noticed that one person was trying to jump down from the bridge. He stopped his bike and approached the person who was trying to jump. "Hey man what are doing?" He replied, "I am fad up of my life and wish to live no more, let me jump and die." The first man told him, "hey you listen to me for five minutes and thereafter if you still wish to commit suicide you can jump from the bridge." They had debate and discussion for ten minutes and after ten minutes both of them jumped from the bridge and committed suicide. The first man tried to convince the second one about the value of life but the second one convinced the first one that your life is also useless.

Fault Finding Attitude

A couple was living in a flat. Wife used to curse the lady living in the other apartment for not being able to wash clothes properly. She used to tell her husband by looking through the front window, "How bad she washes her clothes, how dirty they are looking." Few days later when she stares at the window and notices something different, she immediately calls her husband and says, "Look honey, I think she has heard our discussion, today she has washed clothes properly. They are looking very clean." Husband responded "Darling, actually I have cleaned the glass of our window and that's why clothes are looking clean.

People who have fault finding attitude always in search of faults in others. They are experts in finding faults in best of the persons, best of the situations and best of the things, whereas they need corrections in themselves.

Identify your attitude:

Just watch your habits and actions you can easily determine what kind of attitude you have. If you accept responsibility willingly, you are sincere and disciplined towards your life and action, if you praise people and abstain from criticizing and complaining, if you are punctual and manage your affairs in efficient manner. You don't feel jealous of others progress. You help people growing. You encourage people and you smile often. You have control on your temper. You are optimistic about future events which are beyond your control. If all this happening to you, you have perfect attitude and amidst all challenges and adversities you have all chances of going a long way in your life. But be careful if you have habit of criticizing, complaining, looking at people with suspicion, escaping from responsibility, procrastinating, casual approach towards life, discouraging people, noticing negative part of somebody's personality, making fun of others. These all ensure that you have negative mindset and its going to affect your life, business, growth, family, relationship, health and overall environment.

If you want to grow and want all round success in your life inculcate right attitude. I know it's not easy to change attitude but you have no other choice but to change.

Your close friends and colleagues can also help you knowing about the kind of changes you should bring in to your thoughts.

Surprisingly, many people despite having wrong attitude are not aware of this fact. If you are interested in knowing about your attitude, then see the following checklist:

- Do you escape from taking any responsibility?
- Do you procrastinate?
- Do you indulge in criticizing people in your conversations?
- Do you complain about the system, society and rituals?
- Do you avoid accepting your mistakes?
- Are you undisciplined, having not control over your time and action?
- Are you suffering from the disease called "ME"?
- Do you feel jealous of others success and growth?
- Do you take credit for the work which you didn't accomplish?
- Are you too much self centered?
- Do you escape from helping your friends when they need it?
- Do you keep the feeling of hatred for long and don't forgive easily?
- Do you look at people with suspicion?
- Do you avoid doing self analysis?
- Do you blame people for your problems or failures?

- Do you don't regret or feel shame for your own mistakes?

If your most answers are positive, it's alarming and you must take an immediate corrective action. You are suffering from Negative attitude disease and it's a big hindrance in your way.

Now see the following checklist:

- Do you accept responsibility willingly?
- Do you trust people generally and try to learn something from them?
- Do you have control on your schedule and actions?
- Do you set targets and goals and keep a track on them?
- Do you appreciation people and give constructive criticism?
- Do you believe in finishing task today if it's doable?
- Do you accept your mistakes and learn from them?
- Do you think for self and others as well and believe in creating a win-win situation?
- Do you share the credit of the work done by you and your team?
- Do you use word "WE" more rather than "ME?
- Do you feel happy with others success and take inspiration from it?
- Do you co-operate and help people?
- Do you have a self improvement plan?

If answer to most of the above questions is positive, GREAT you have a fabulous, positive and fantastic attitude. It will definitely take you to your destiny.

ATTITUDE is reflection of yours:

1. It ensures success or failure: If you face challenges and problems you take it sportingly and challenge them if you have positive mindset otherwise you give up easily and make sure that you will not cope with it up.
2. It defines our approach towards life: You are very specific, disciplined and systematic or you are casual, living in urgency addicted life style, you take life very easily and you have no plans or ambitions in life. Your attitude defines your approach and that takes you to two different roads, a road which takes you nowhere and a road which takes you to your dream destination.
3. It scripts the strength of your relationships: You easily make relationship, nurture them and maintain them or you stand aloof and fail to maintain relationship. Certainly "your attitude determines the fate of your relationships". You appreciate, co-operate and encourage people or you curse, criticize and take them for granted, choice is yours. Your attitude will certainly script it.
4. It affects your health: You have positive mindset, you stay happy and you often smile and feel happy with others success. If you have fear, jealousy and anxiety they are results of your negative attitude. Both different situations will produce different results. Good health or bad health. Choice is yours.

5. Finally it affects your growth: Having positive attitude ensures that you grow with a consistent pace whereas negative attitude ensures that you will not reach your goal, you will struggle and blame others or situation for your failures.

Attitude of Living with the Solution

You're either living in the problem or you're living with the solution. Find out where you are and just mould your attitude to the right lane. Always try to be on the side of solution. So, try to provide solutions to your problems yourself. Bear in mind -

To the question of your life you are the answer, and to the problems of your life you are the solution.

- Joe Cordare

Attitude of not quitting:

When problems and defeat overtake a person, the easiest and most logical thing seems to him, is to QUIT. That is exactly what the majority of people do. But do remember one thing always – each barrier and problem coming to your way is a stepping-stone towards success.

Here's a story –

Strong Will Power

If a man has a strong will power & a killer instinct, then he can even come over the death. This story depicts such qualities of a soldier who fought in a War & displayed extraordinary valour by killing 10 soldiers of enemy. He very narrowly escaped from the death. While fighting, the bullet penetrated into his body & his heart saved from a margin. When he was hospitalized, after undergoing many tests and scans, the doctors had told him that he was no longer going to be alive.

But he was not ready to give up so easily. As usual, he was going through the routine check up, suddenly he asked for a hundred-rupee note. The doctor was standing nearby & offered him the note. But he refused to accept it from him.

He asked the doctor to get his wallet & took out a hundred-rupee note from it & betted doctor that he will certainly live & asked him to do his surgery. The doctor was amazed to see such a strong will power of a patient whose death was at the next door. Without delay the doctors did the surgery. There is a saying "All is well that ends well", surgery was successful.

This instance makes us realize that we should never loose our hope & should strive till the end to face any situation.

Besides, The Magic is in YOU!

The cause of the confusion prevailing in your mind that weakens your thoughts and the root cause of your delayed success is the false belief that there is a power or powers outside you greater than the power within you. Remember there's no power in this world stronger than you and your inner strength. All you have to make is to believe it and act accordingly.

What is more, one should always bear in mind the sentence -

"Even if he fails again and again to accomplish his purpose — as he must until weakness is overcome — the strength of character gained will be the measure of his true success, and this will form a new starting point for future power and triumph."

- As A Man Thinketh

What you Say is What You GET

We focus a lot on how powerful our thoughts and actions are and in so doing, we overlook one of the most powerful killers of dreams — our words.

Sentences reflecting negative attitude -

It's not my fault I am the way I am.

I never asked to be born.

My parents did nothing for me.

Life is unfair! There is no sense in trying to take control of my life.

Why go on; I see no use in it.

You can't help me, nobody can help me. I'm useless and a failure.

God has asked too much of me this time. There is no way I'll ever be able to handle this. When do the troubles and problems cease? I'm tired of all this.

Life is so depressing. If only I had better luck and had been born to a healthier family, or attended a better school, or gotten a better job

How can you say I am responsible for what happens to me in the future? There is fate, luck, politics, greed, envy, wicked and jealous people, and other negative influences that have a greater bearing on my future than I have.

How can I ever be happy, seeing how bad my life has been?

My parents made me what I am today!

The problems in my family have influenced who I am and what I will be; there is nothing I can do to change that.

No matter how hard I work, I will never get ahead.

It's simple. Some people are born lucky. I was not.

I am who I am; there is no changing me.

The stars are against me.

So, how many of them were applicable to you? All of them? or A few? Or None?

They all signify the feelings of a person who refuses to accept the responsibility for himself.

These statements depict that how easily man tends to let go things out of his hands. Though he can take the ownership of his actions, he can guide his own thought process, he can question back his own statements and remarks, yet it seems simpler to remark negatively.

Have a vocabulary that inspires. The words that you use are the vibrations you instil in your surrounding environment. Appreciating, pleasing and positive vocabulary not only guides your mind in the positive direction but also influences everyone around.

In his infinite wisdom, God did not make any of us perfect. For all happiness, there is a sorrow and for every smile there is a tear. The most beautiful person in the world has maybe a terrible voice or no brains!

Learn to Accept

Somebody rightly said "The God has given them everything because they had trust in the God. The God has given me nothing because the God had trust in me."

Accept the following to resolve your attitude into a positive one -

- Accept that life is not about finding the right person, but about carrying on a right relationship.

- Accept that life is not about getting a perfect pal, but about loving an imperfect pal perfectly.
- Accept that your desires have no end and that your means will never match your desires.
- Accept that all the money in the world can only buy you pleasure but not happiness
- Accept that your physical body has endurance limits although your mind may not.
- Accept that you are responsible for what you choose to feel or think.
- Accept that you choose the direction for your life.
- Accept that you cannot blame others for the choices you have made.
- Accept that you are your best motivator; it is not reasonable or healthy for you to depend on others to make you feel good about yourself.
- Accept that you are responsible for protecting and nurturing your health and emotional well being.
- Accept that only you have to structure your life with factors like time management, anger management, stress management, confronting fears, and burnout prevention
- Accept that the generation gap between you and your kids will seem greater than the one between you and your parents
- Accept the dictum - the smaller the man, the bigger is his ego

If you do not accept the above, you run the risk of being: -

- Overly dependent on other people for recognition and approval.
- Forever angry or depressed over how unfairly you have been or are being treated.
- Fearful about ever taking a risk or making a decision.
- Unsuccessful at the enterprises you take on in life.
- Unsuccessful in your personal and social relationships.

Learn to accept and know what is acceptance-

Acceptance

Acceptance means that you
Can find the serenity within
to let go of the past
with its mistakes and regrets,
move into the future
with a new perspective,
and appreciate the opportunity
to take a second chance.
Acceptance means you'll find
Security again
When difficult times come
Into your life,
And comfort to relieve any pain.
You'll find new dreams, fresh hopes,
And forgiveness of the heart.
Acceptance does not mean
that you will always be perfect.
It simply means that
you'll always overcome imperfection.
Acceptance is the road to peace-

Letting go of the worst,
Holding on to the best,
and finding the hope inside
that continues throughout life.
Acceptance
is the heart's best defence,
Love's greatest asset,
and the easiest way
to keep believing
in yourself and others.

-Author unknown

Consistent Positive Attitude

When confronted with a difficult situation, a person with an outstanding attitude makes the best of fit while he gets the worst of it.

With a positive attitude, you will have the ability to be happier each day, make others around you happier, and live a good life. Below are few tips that can help you keeping your positive attitude growing.

1. **Put Things in Perspective**

   When you find your mood is taking a turn for the worse, take a step back and put things into perspective. Is the stress and frustration really worth it? When you look at the bigger picture, don't they seem a bit insignificant? They should, because nine times out of ten the daily problems we face are not really that important when we look at life as a whole. You are alive; you have food, shelter, and freedom. These things are reason enough to smile when you wake in the morning.

2. **Have Something to Look Forward To**

   You are expecting something in the mail. Then, finally, it comes! People love to look forward to things. Some say that anticipation of something happening is better than when it actually happens. We all have special events that are coming up. Holidays, birthdays, vacations, weekends, etc. Keeping these in mind will give you something to stay excited about.

3. **Help Others**

   There is no better way to forget about your worries than to help someone else with theirs. When you take the focus off yourself, and give your attention to helping people, your attitude will change dramatically. This tip not only includes helping friends and family, but also volunteering to help those in need that you may not know. When you give of yourself, you will receive tenfold in return.

4. **Take a Break**

   There are times when the only solution is to get away from it all. If you know that you are in a negative mood, or have been in low spirits for some time, take a break. It could be just what you need. Taking a break can vary from a short trip to a vacation. A walk around the neighbourhood can also work wonders for your mood and attitude.

5. **Talk with a Positive Friend**

   Talking things out can help you see the good in a bad situation. Call a friend and tell them about your problem, or just chat about any topic that comes to you. This is a very therapeutic and effective cure to a rough day.

6. **Life is Short**

   One thing to always remember is that life is short. The worst thing would be to look back on your days wishing you could have been happier. Now is the time to take a good look at your attitude and make the necessary improvements. Days, weeks, months, and years have a way of rushing by. Do not let them pass while you are in a negative mood about life. Look back with no regrets, only happy memories.

7. **People Have Done More With Less**

   A common cause for a poor attitude is the feeling that, you are in a situation that is just too hard to deal with. People have done more with less. Many people from all over the world have overcome obstacles, solved problems, and maintained a positive attitude through the most tiring of times. If they can do it, so can you.

   The power of a positive attitude is always within your reach. You simply have to extend your hand and grab it.

Use the tips above to gain a great attitude, and to make your life happier, healthier, and wealthier.

Story: Close your tap of negativity:

Once I was conducting a seminar on confidence building. During the break one participant approached me and told "Sir I want to discuss my personal problem with me". I listened to him. He told" Sir I have a very low confidence, I can't speak confidently, I can't communicate properly, I feel shy meeting new people, I feel scared, what should I Do?"

After listening to him I narrated him a small and real incidence of my life. Many years back when I was in college,

I had a habit of going for jogging in the morning. It was cold wintry morning, I got up around 6 in the morning got ready and got down on the ground floor. The moment I jumped from the last step to the floor, the logged water got splashed on me and I got wet. I saw that lot of water logged on the floor. I immediately took the wiper and started clearing water. After lot of efforts the water level remained same, suddenly my mother also got down and yelled at me. "What the hell you are doing Pritam in the morning." I told "Mom I am clearing water for last ten minutes but water level is not getting down." My mom said, "Before doing that just switch the tap off which is releasing continuous water." I laughed on myself, switched off the tap and within few seconds the whole water was gone out of the floor. I further told that guy, listen gentleman, if you want to be confident and daring just put your tap of negativity which is there at the back of your head. Unless you have the right and positive attitude and keep on thinking and uttering negative about yourself, you can't succeed in gaining the desired confidence.

Formation of Attitude

There are many factors which help forming an attitude.

- There is inherent temperament which is inherited to us by our parents.
- Family atmosphere.
- Our friends and social network.
- Education, both formal and informal.
- Our experiences in life.

Sometime two persons getting nurtured in a common environment develop different kind of attitude due to different temperament. Like two brothers nurtured in a family under same environment but one has good habits and other has bad ones.

Actually what we hear, watch and speak all through the day, contribute to our temperament. I am really impressed with the three monkeys of Mahatma Gandhi. Monkeys covering eyes, mouth and ears, symbolizes that one should abstain himself / herself looking at bad things, listening to negative or bad things and speaking bad things. By doing so, we stay away from negative influences in life, and able to keep our mind and soul positive.

Self Images Matters a Lot

In the very first chapter I have explained in detail what is self image? So far as attitude is concerned self image plays a vital role.

If you have a self image of confused, shaky, unconfident, unsecured person it will lead you to a situation where you will have a negative attitude. If you have a positive self image, belief in your own abilities slowly and gradually you will form a positive and constructive attitude in life.

Changing the Bad attitude

If you really want to change your destiny, want to grow rapidly, want yourself to be recognized as a good human being, want to develop good relationships, just look at your attitude. You need to introspect and find out the areas of improvement.

Remember it's too hard to change the attitude, but you can certainly change it if you really want to change it. Here are few steps you should take to bring that positive change to your life:

1. **Set Goals and have vision and mission in life:**

   I have seen many people leading life without purpose. They get up and go to work. They come back and go to bed. It brings stagnancy to your life. You should have clearly defined goals, a mission and a clear vision in your life, which continues to be a source of inspiration for you and every moment in life you wish to step forward and achieve mile stone one after another.

2. **Expose to New situations and opportunities:**

   You should try new ways to do work, new dishes to eat, new choices of clothes. If you get new opportunities you should accept them. Exposing to new situations and opportunities is going to make your mind set big and wide and leads towards positive approach.

3. **Expand your friends and social network:**

   The more people you meet and know the more knowledge and better attitude you have. A negative person can't gel with so many people, doesn't enjoy having more friends. It not only helps becoming positive but also helps in making progress in your profession. The more people you know the more sense of acceptability you will have.

4. **Enhance your learning, read good books:**

   Keep learning new things. Learn from different people you meet, learn from every opportunity you get or situation you are into and enjoy learning. Reading good books regularly is going to expand your horizon. Even if you have less time read at least 5 to 10 pages of a book, this way you can easily read 10-15 books in a year and you will realize 5 years down the line how much knowledge and wisdom you have gathered in this process. But remember the selection of books is very important. You can read management, motivational, professional books or periodicals and journals.

5. **Plan your day and follow the schedule:**

   You should have total control on your daily schedule. If everything goes in a planned manner you are more productive which ultimately fills you with positivism. You need to define your day, have defined time slot for your activities and keep some provision for contingencies too.

6. **Take responsibilities:**

   You should be willing to take more responsibilities at home, office, college or in social organizations. Feel happy when people entrust you with responsibilities. More responsibilities you take the better leader and performer you become which finally makes you positive.

7. **Indulge in some social activities:**

   The world, nature, society and the country have given us a lot. We should give some time to some social activities without any self interest. Once we start to have the feeling of giving or sacrificing, it gives lots of positive energy.

8. **Appreciate people for their efforts:**

   Whenever you see somebody doing a good task, develop a habit of appreciating the same on the spot. This will not only create a different kind of happiness within you but also make you popular among the people.

9. **Feel happy with others growth and congratulate them:**

I have seen many people envying with others progress. You should feel happy seeing people growing and having a feeling of jealously is not going to help you any way rather it will going to make us negative. Whenever you see somebody around you accomplishing something, feel good, take a step forward and congratulate or applaud the person for that achievement.

10. **Always think for a win-win situation:**

    While dealing with people in various situations, try to create a situation where you and the other person have a winning situation. If you only think for your own advantage you tend to go bit negative in your thinking and action.

11. **Don't procrastinate, take actions and initiatives earliest:**

    When you already know the task you need to do then why to postpone it on other day. This approach makes you sluggish and dull. Take initiatives and actions to your earliest. The task which is doable today must not be shifted on tomorrow.

12. **Spend more time with positive, inspiring and growing individuals:**

    Your company makes a lot of difference to your life. You should spend maximum of your time with those who are positive, a source of inspiration and progressing in their lives. You will certainly get a reflection on your personality.

13. **Convert fear into faith:**

    Fears make you negative. It creates anxiety and generates a sense of insecurity. Having a fear is not going to help you anyway. Just have faith on yourself and you are not paying any cost of having faith instead of fear. Fear of failure, fear of losing a friend or client, fear of child going on wrong track etc.

14. **Change your vocabulary:**

    You must eliminate certain words from your dictionary. I can't, I doubt, I don't know, I am afraid, What if, I don't believe, I don't have time, I am helpless, Its impossible. Try to minimize word "I" from your conversations. Substitute these words with positive ones like "Ya I can, I trust, I am capable of, We will, it's possible, I am confident, Let's hope for the best etc.

15. **Leave Bad habits:**

    You need to watch your habits of getting up late, going to bed late, smoking, drinking, telling a lie, eating without discipline or not taking care of health, wasting too much time with friends in unproductive things. You should have a plan of getting rid of these habits.

    Knowing what you didn't know, doing what you didn't know makes you get what you haven't got. Realize flaws in your attitude, change it into positive one and sky is the limit for you. You will never look back and life will yield you handsome profits.

5

Dreams to Destination

(Goal Setting and Accomplishment)

Imagine! You ask few children to play football in a ground. They start playing and their parents and friends reach there to watch the game. All the players are running after the ball and kicking it whenever they are getting the chance. They are excited and thrilled. One or two of them are fast they are getting more chances to kick; few others are running after it but getting few chance. After 10-15 minutes some of them stop running, few of them have already disassociated from this fun. Few are still in it but the enthusiasm level is low and excitement is also going down.

Some more time passes; many of them are now just standing in the field, neither running nor trying to get the ball. If the ball automatically comes to them, they kick it haywire and those who run after it, they laugh at them. Even the spectators have started losing their interest.

Now some one gets up and fixes a set of poles at both the ends of the ground and announces that "Guys these are the GOALS for you". Now you can notice the rapid swing in the moods and excitement level of the players. Their faces are radiant again. By this time the kids have divided themselves into two groups. You are silently watching. The real game begins now. Everyone starts putting hundred percent, they are focused and target oriented. Despite of reduction in energy level no one is willing to give up. They are more serious about the game now. They are having fun but with a great amount of responsibility and commitment.

One team scores a goal. Spectators on the fence start clapping automatically. Kids who could not score are more charged now. They are shouting with passion. Their supporters outside are also shouting to motivate them they are just seeing only two things, the ball and the goal. Every moment the excitement is mounting.

You still sitting on the fence, amused to the see the power of those set of sticks you called GOALS.

Yes! They are amazing. It is the GOALS in the playfield that generates fun filled game with a PURPOSE. It is only the GOALS that give you energy to perform and to outperform the rivals. It's only the Goals that bring your friends and relative to your support. It is the goals that give direction to every action of yours and whenever you are wrong, your co-players and supporters remind you. Goals give focus to you direction and slowly make it sharp laser focused. Goals make you achievement motivated. Even a small success on your way towards goal gives you immense satisfaction. No game without goals can produce Ronaldo, Pele, Maradona or Beckham. And no hero can bring excitement in the game without goals. It is power of goals in the game that glues millions and millions of spectators to TV screen and push people to spend fortunes on games. The beauty of every playfield is GOALS.

So is the playfield of life. Like no game is a game without goals, No life is life without a goal. This goal (goals) is the Purpose for which we live a meaningful life, having satisfaction, happiness, and sense of achievement or sense of having done something worthwhile. It brings the people around us closer to us, supporting us, motivating us, and many a time, sharing the action also. Life becomes an activity with a Reason.

"Life without a Reason is a sequence of useless events"

I see very few people on the earth who achieved what they aspired or dreamt. Each one of us dreamt since our birth, but how many of those dreams are attained? Very few.. or almost none. But there are people almost 1 in 1000 who decide what they have to do, where they have to reach, when they have to reach and how they have to reach and they do what they think. As a human being you must have a purpose to live and one should strive hard to attain that purpose. A goal less life is like a boat in the sea without the rudder. It goes nowhere instead it's controlled by the waves of the sea itself. If you don't have goal or aim in your life your life is certainly be under total command of prevailing circumstances else you can control all circumstances by having goals and conviction for those goals.

Goal setting is a plan of action which leads to a number of activities in a sequential order which end with an achievement. Once you set your goal and decide your aim you will know the course of action you have to take because you know the complete road map and priorities of your life.

Why People Fail?

I have seen people planning so many things in life. People plan their attire, trips, parties but most of them forget to plan their lives. Rather they keep on postponing the task of planning their lives. They seem to be very casual about the life. If you fail to plan you are certainly planning your failure. If you don't have clear picture in your mind you will certainly go here and there under the state of confusion. I have seen many people taking wrong decisions and changing them afterwards. Someone has rightly said "Life is a drawing without an eraser." You can't reverse your decisions, which you took in the past. Even if you reverse you can't get your time, money, efforts and energy which you spent with the old decision. And that's the reason why people don't reach where they should have reached. If you want to be different from a common or ordinary man, if you want to reach to your destination, start searching your true destination and make a concrete time bound plan to act on it.

Life is Full of Challenges

Life is full of challenges. Especially in today's global scenario nothing is static. One has to keep growing every time. It's indeed a "Do or Die" world. You either progress or you perish! There is no more any mere survival for passive thinkers and stagnant people. Undoubtedly the world is full of opportunities but those are really not easily available to everyone.

Gone are the days when the ***doers*** were limited. The scope for someone, despite being mediocre, wanting to attain something was a possibility. Now it's altogether different scenario. Every second person is your competitor. Look at the time which was prevailing 30 years back when scoring 75% marks in school exams used to be a great achievement but now it is considered a mediocre one. Have a look at the world of sports where records are broken almost every day which were created in 100 years.

At what level you are standing today? What is your brand image?, Whether you will be able to sustain the current progress in the future? Are you sure of making a significant position of yourself in life. You have already spent a considerable time and the time ahead is very limited.

It's time to get ready for the future, It's either now or never situation. Today's scenario is demanding to aim big with passion and to do everything with one hundred percent focus.

Discovering the Aim

It's an exercise in which you will discover broad, personal life goals. Like many of us, you may not be conscious of your own priorities or realize the importance of this step. Virtually all our actions relate directly to efforts to accomplish our life goals. Our work, family and social life goals are deeply intertwined. If we are unaware of our broader goals and why we behave the way we do in any given situation, we act more consistently to accomplish them.

We have listed (in alphabetical order) the broader life goals people frequently identify. To clarify your priorities, rank the items on this list in terms of your own values.

First, rank the goals listed from one to ten in the order of importance i.e. most important to least important.

Second, go back and think about them comprehensively. This will help you look at yourself in terms of your life goals.

If you have important goals not listed here, add them to the list and give them your own definition. If you disagree with the broad definition of any of the goals below, substitute your own.

- *Affection* To obtain and share companion ship and affection through immediate family and friends.
- *Commitment* To dedicate myself totally to the pursuit of values and ideals.
- *Expertise* To become an authority on a special subject and to reach an expert level of skill and accomplishment.
- *Independence* To have an opportunity for freedom of thought and action; to be my own boss.
- *Leadership* To become an influential leader and to organize and direct others to achieve social or organizational goals.
- *Pleasure* To enjoy life, to be happy, to have fun and to have the good things in life.
- *Recognition* To become well- known, to obtain recognition, awards and better life standards.
- *Security* To achieve a secure and stable position in work and financially.
- *Self* – realizations to optimize personal development, to realize my full creative and innovative potential.
- *Service* To contribute to the needs, satisfaction, and development of others, to be helpful to others.
- *Wealth To earn or to have a great deal of money.*
- ....
- ....

The Burning Desire Within

The Process of Goal setting and its attainment starts with the burning desire which doesn't let you sit quiet, idle and calm.

I have seen thousands of people complaining and blaming their destiny or luck for failures and debacles in their lives. Most of them believe that success of this life is the result of good luck or deeds of previous life. I honestly believe that all humans have the power to change the destiny.

Many of us see an air craft flying in the sky each day and we all know the science behind the plane flying and we still feel amazed to imagine a heavy piece of equipment flying. Well, this invention just did not happen. We all know that the Wright Brothers had to go through numerous failures and embarrassment before they could create a plane that could fly. Were they destined to create a plane? Was it their fate that got them to create a plane? I doubt.

It was their observation of the birds and the desire to fly which made them create the machine which is called an aircraft now. It was their burning desire which was so strong that made them work for years and hours each day before they met with success. When Wright brothers were in the process of inventing an airplane, the U.S. president commented on them ***"A human being can never fly. He would have born with wings, if he was supposed to"***. Even this time of negative comments could not shake the confidence of Wright brothers and we all know they could convert their dream into reality despite so many failures. All the failures, taunts, embarrassment and frustration were small compared to their burning desire to fly. It is only through a Burning Desire can a man achieves the impossible.

Obstacles come and it is up to us how we deal with them. Failures will come for a long time, before we can achieve something. It is the manner in which the Universe functions. To reap fruits from a tree, you must first plant the seeds and nurture the tree well.

Achieving anything is possible as long as you have the Burning Desire to achieve it, i.e. creating the next scientific experiment, topping your exams, receiving the next promotion, losing your weight, learning a new art. Anything is possible. The recent slogan of 'Adidas' says it all "Impossible is nothing".

Law of attraction says, "If you have a Burning Desire and sow the seeds of intention, the universe conspires to help you". This happens only if your intentions are true and pure.

If you dream of achieving something then sow the seeds of intention in the universe by always being positive about that dream and always thinking of that dream, the universe will conspire to help you. You might dream to work in New York and if you sow your intentions right, somewhere somehow you might just bump into a person who could help you.

Therefore, keep dreaming, always have the burning desire to succeed and read the following steps to achieve your goals. But remember, it requires a disciplined approach and complete dedication while following it.

Commandments for Goal Setting

Please note that the steps mentioned below require a sincere and disciplined approach. By discipline I mean that no matter what difficulty you face in achieving your goals, you must stick to your desire to achieving your goals.

1. **Look into the Value System**

   What's really important to you? Your Business? Your family? Your religion? Your leisure time? Or Your hobbies? Decide on what your most important values in life are and then make sure that the goals you set are designed to include and enhance them.

2. **Begin with the End in Mind**

   Tom Watson, the founder of IBM was once asked what he attributed the phenomenal success of IBM to and he said they were three things:

   The first thing was that he created a very clear image in his mind of what he wanted his company to look like when it was done. He then asked himself, how would a company like that have to act on a day-to-day basis? And then in the very beginning of building his company, he began to act that way.

3. **Future Projection of yourself**

   "We Become What We Think About." Therefore make a projection of yourself where you want to see yourself 20 years down the line.

   Whatever thoughts dominate our minds, most of the time they are what we become. That's why goal setting is so critical in achieving success because it keeps us focused on what's really important to us. The easiest way to reach our goals is to pretend that we have ALREADY achieved our goals.

   That is, begin to walk, talk and act as if we are already experiencing the success we seek. Then, those things will come to us naturally through the power of the subconscious mind.

4. **Write priorities of upcoming year**

   By making a list of the things that are important to you, you begin to create images in your mind. It's been said that your mind will actually create chaos if necessary to make images or say dreams become a reality. Because of this, the list of ten things will probably result in you achieving at least eight of them within the forthcoming year.

5. **Create Your Dream chart**

   Get a blank chart paper and fix it to a wall in your office or home where you will be seeing it often. As you go through magazines, brochures, etc. and you see the pictures of the things you want, cut them out and glue them to your dream chart.

   In other words, make yourself a collage of the goals that excite you knowing it well that as you look at them every day, they will soon be yours. This is a very successful technique I have implemented on thousands of students where during the workshop on goal setting we help students making their dream charts. I have plenty of such examples where those students converted those dreams into realities and they give credit to their respective charts.

6. **Top Three items**

   You may have hundreds of things to do in your life time, I don't say you can't but prioritizing them will help you attaining important things first. Decide on three things that you want to achieve before you die. Then work backwards listing three things you want in the next twenty years, ten years, five years, this year, this month, this week and finally, the three most important things you want to accomplish today.

A young girl used to talk about stars and the sky since her childhood. She always dreamt of going into the sky. She used to aspire of becoming something which explores the world of space for her. She was from a middle class family and a small town with no apparent opportunities in the relevant field. But with that dream she had a plan and vision. She was the only girl in Punjab University in "Aeronautical Engineering" branch in that year. She stood firm by her dreams and finally Kalpana Chawla became the first Indian woman to reach NASA. Friends if we have desire deep inside and that desire is converted into plan and that plan is broken into small pieces of daily, weekly and monthly actions no power in this world can stop you achieving your goals.

7. Ask Yourself Good Questions

As you think about your goals, instead of WISHING for them to come true, ask yourself HOW and WHAT CAN YOU DO? to make them come true. The subconscious mind will respond to your questions far greater than just making statements or making wishes. Keep your question meter always ON so that you keep on anticipating what to do next.

8. Focus on One thing At a Time

One of the greatest mistakes people make in setting goals is trying to work on too many things at one time. There is tremendous power in giving laser beam focused attention to just one idea, one project or one objective at a time. Therefore be focused on what you do because you can do one thing at a time and not concentrating on it will result in less productive results.

9. **Depict the "Ideal Scenario"**

   Pretend that you are a newspaper reporter who has just finished an interview about the outstanding success that you've achieved and the article is now in the newspaper. How would it read? What would be the headline? Write the article yourself and projecting yourself into the future, as if it had already happened. Describe the activities of your daily routine now that are very successful. This is indeed a powerful tool to boost the morale and reinforce the belief in ones goals.

10. **Be ready for the adversities:**

    Whatever you do problems are surely going to emerge your way. It depends how you take those problems and manage them. It would be a better idea to perceive all such situations well in advance and have readymade plan to combat with that problem. Otherwise every time you are going to be surprised with every such situation and may be after few such instances you will lose the way. Remember, nothing comes easy. Even a diamond has to go through endless pressure and heat to reach its final form.

    It's how we react to problems that make all the difference. Many things will come your way and distract your mind and that's the time to keep yourself cool, composed and keep driving on.

11. **Keep track of your progress**

    After defining the goal, initiating the action and battling with lots of adversities which come your way; it's time to monitor your progress.

    The reason why you should monitor your progress is to know if the action that you have initiated is helping you to near your goals or not. If you feel that the action is not helping you much, then you should try to alter your path of working. May be you were doing it all wrong. Don't panic at this stage. Appreciate the knowledge that you have gained of how not to achieve your goal. That's experience.

12. Find a mentor

Very few people have the privilege of being guided by a mentor. If you wish to become an entrepreneur, a scientist, a singer or a dancer, then seek the help of a mentor. The experience of a mentor will not only lead you through a correct path, but will also help you become the best in an apt time frame.

13. Pray & Meditate

As you get into bed each evening, think about your goal before you drop off to sleep. Get a very clear colorful image in your mind of seeing yourself doing the things you'll be doing after you've reached your major goal. And then begin to ask and demand for these things through meditation and prayer.

Thomas Edison had to go through thousands of failed experiments to achieve the goal of inventing the perfect light bulb that we use today. At a press conference when he was asked about his failures, he quickly responded saying "I have successfully discovered 10000 ways to NOT make a light bulb". Then what happened later on, he became the only scientist who had more than 900 patents registered in his own name. What if he had given up in first few trials??

This shows that he had a goal and a burning desire to build an electric bulb. This proves that despite facing so many problems and failed attempts he kept on trying with different ideas which made him to achieve creating the first electrical bulb ever witnessed by mankind.

Writing Your Goals

First of all make an inventory of whatever you want to attain in your life in terms of skills, assets, money, health, relationships, image, recognition etc. Now classify them into three categories viz. Short term goals which are to be attained in next couple of years, Middle term goals which are to be attained in next 5-7 years and long term goals which are to be attained in next 10-15 years. There may be life time goals also which you want to attain across your life. You must take care while framing your short term and middle term goals as they must be aligned with the long term goals. Your today's action is going to contribute in attainment of your middle and long term goal and later short term and middle term goals become the foundation for your long term goals, so that not even a single goal of your life should be unrelated with any of your middle or long term goal.

Once you categorize your goals prioritize Short-term goals to achieve your life goals. If your life goals require you to fulfill a number of objectives or short – term goals, those objectives or short – term goals should be prioritized so that you can concentrate on the most useful or the most helpful at any given time.

Your goals statement must express your goals clearly.

Follow these suggestions as closely as possible.

1. *Start the goal statement with an infinitive.*

   A goal is not a "good resolution". Goals are action oriented.

The infinitive in English begins with the word "to"

To lead…

To earn..

To own…

To score..

To write…

2. *State clearly what you want to achieve.* A goal states what a person will do, by planned action, to bring it about.
3. *Be specific as possible.* Make a goal measurable. To achieve a goal, people need to know precisely what they want. It's not enough to want to improve, they must specify how much and in what area they will improve. Instead of saying "To improve profit is my goal," they specify *what* they will do and *how much.* The easiest way to make a goal measurable is to put numbers in the goal statement or to determine a specific standard of performance.
4. *Make a goal realistic* sometimes people set goals they cannot achieve. Goals must be practical and possible. The potential resources of the organization in terms of people, time and finances are the limits within which people set organizational goals. In the case of personal goals; people need to move away from setting unrealistic goals they cannot reasonably expect to achieve.
5. *Make goals challenging* Too idealistic goals lead to frustration. Too easily reached goals fail to create enthusiasm. Challenging goals demand

improvement on present performances. People need goals that challenge, have something to learn or to improve their skills in the process of achieving them. Challenging goals require that people become more effective than they were in the past.

6. *Set the date-* undated goals usually remain unattained. Terminated dates forces people into action, to get things done for self-development or the good of the organization. That's the whole purpose of goal setting! They must set specific time period rather than randomly direct their energies toward some vague point in the future. If they set a time limit of a month or a year on the goal, thus places a constraint on them. They know they must take action to achieve the goal within the established time period. If they have no time target, how will they measure their progress?
7. *Write the goals* –'Goals not written get forgotten'. Without written reminders, most people forget to "do it today" or to "try it a little harder". Writing it down *commits* people and they are more likely to achieve a goal they have written out than one they only think about

Take the Action

"You must take action now that will move you towards your goals. Develop a sense of urgency in your life." - Les Brown

Now that you have created a goal for yourself, the next step is to initiate action and work towards it by giving all efforts possible. This is the most difficult part in achieving a goal. Many of my students and colleagues have some goals, but they failed at the most critical step i.e. when to initiate action.

After your goals are clear, the time to take action is NOW. Just start working towards it. Ask yourself if you'd be happy to achieve your goals? If yes, then why don't you start working towards it in spite of having a clear vision of your goal? If your goal is to lose weight, then the next logical step is to find out how you could achieve it. Join a gym, consult a doctor, Fix a diet plan etc. Just do everything possible towards achieving your goal.

"Well done is always better than well said"

Goals! How big they may be and how great they may sound are just fantasies if they are not followed by ACTION.

"Performance is the crux"

No success is possible without a planned activity you do for it. Action alone attracts achievements, big or small!

We all have potential to perform but most of the times we get satisfied with the performance that gives us some success or small achievement. There comes the time when one should start focusing to the long term goals (the most challenging ones) that we discussed while writing and categorizing our goals. Challenging goals are always demanding, the action required to conquer them is not ordinary ones. They have to be the best planned and executed in the best flawless manner. We all have the potential to do that; only thing is to be able to perform as per our potential.

Many a times, we hesitate performing because of an unseen fear of failure. We shirk the required risk in the activity. That something unforeseen scares us and we decide not to perform.

Remember:

"The person, who risks nothing, does nothing, gets nothing and finally ends up nothing."

"There are two kinds of people who never amount too much.

Those who cannot do what they are supposed to do'

Others who can do nothing else"

To a goal well determined, it is not possible to reach without a plan and then, that plan needs to be executed. Most of the people fail to act because they start seeing the big mountain of work ahead. To begin it is only a one single step initiated in the right direction. Do not see the big bulge of task ahead try and initiate small beginning, small but continuous action toward your target. Ask everyday what I did and what is the achievement. The small amount of success you get everyday will motivate you for further bigger actions and finally you will end up scaling high mountains, which were scaring you in the very beginning. It is learning to eat elephant. Cut it to pieces and finish a piece at a time. You will get a few failures. You will be hurt at times but your strong determination and faith in your goal will get you going.

"It is a shallow life that does not give a few scars"

- Kiran Bedi

I read a news column in The Times of India few years back that son of tea stall owner scored 34th rank in Indian Civil services examinations. How did it happen? The Answer is very clear the dreams and aspirations were converted into systematic plan and all the fears and inferiorities were kept aside. When I look at so many other students who have sound academic background, toppers in their schools and colleges, take special coaching for these exams still they fail to achieve what that apparently an ordinary guy achieved.

Most important thing after identifying a goal worthwhile is to DECIDE to act. When you take decision to act nothing can stop you.

"Vital reserves are taped. New levels attained.

Indifference becomes conviction.

Inertia becomes initiative,

When you decide to act."

All the best to you for your journey from unknown to well known. Please do not go back from your decisions. Acting on your decisions makes you a complete human being capable of achieving with HAPPINESS. Once you have started off, you will find that the pieces fall into place and you reach where you wanted to reach and that too with a lot of contentment.

Powerful Lessons

Obstacles are those frightening things that become visible when we take our eyes off our goals.

- Henry Ford

Set your goals high and don't stop until you get there.

- Bo Jackson

You must take action now that will move you towards your goals. Develop a sense of urgency in your life.

- Les Brown

Keep away from people who try to belittle your ambitions. Small people always do that, but the really great make you feel that you, too, can become great.

- Mark Twain

Arise, Awake and Stop not till the goal is reached.

- Swami Vivekanand

"Our goals can only be reached through a vehicle of a plan, in which we must fervently believe, and upon which we must vigorously act. There is no other route to success."

- Stephen A. Brennan

EXERCISE

Your Goal Achievemnt Plan

Select one of your goals and take it through the following steps:

1. The specific goal I wish to accomplish within the next 6-12 months is________________________ ________________________ Make sure that goal is specific, realistic, challenging and measurable.
2. This goal is important to me because______________
3. It relates to my long-term goals in that it__________ ____
4. If I attain it, I will feel ________________________
5. If I do not attain it, I will feel

   ____

   ____
6. I consider the possibility of success to be___________

   ____
7. The obstacles are:

(a) Things: ______________________________

(b) People: ______________________________

8. I plan to overcome these obstacles by:

(a) ______________________________________

____

(b) ______________________________________

____

9. My resources and helps in accomplishing my goal:

(a) Things :______________________________

____

(b) People: ______________________________

____

10. I intend to use these helps by____________________

____

____

11. The specific action steps with time-targets that I intend to take to reach my goals:

(a) Steps: ______________________________

____

____

(b) I will begin by__________________________

____

(c) My time-target date to finish is________________

____

Acknowledgement: ***Goal setting exercises are taken from Antony D'souza's LEADERSHIP***

6

Change is Permanent

CHANGE: The Only Thing in Life, That's The Permanent!

- Anthony Magee

The only thing permanent in this world is change. Change is the rule of nature. Change has pervaded all the phases of life. Change is the key to survive and grow.

Mahatma Gandhi said it so well, "Be the change that you wish to see most in your world, and once you do, your life will change." And the change must begin in our opinionated perceptions and prejudices. Only through questioning our existing thoughts can we move to a higher level of thought process. In our personal life we always try to be a better version today, of what we were yesterday. We always look for a change in ourselves. In order to compete and thrive one has to change. Without change you seem to be out of the counting sphere. It's a "Do or Die" world. You either progress or you perish! There is no more any *mere survival*, or *`let me just stay alone'* scenario prevalent today.

Are You Changing?

Change is inevitable yet it is most difficult thing to implement. The world is changing too fast. Technology is changing rapidly & knowledge too. Almost everything around us is changing with an unpredictable speed.

Once I met a teacher who was teaching geography for many years. She confidently said "I have 20 years experience teaching my subject". I said with a bit correction, "You have one year experience repeated 19 times". She was stunned to listen to this. Unless you do new things or learn new ways, you are not gathering experience rather you are becoming conditioned to old ways, and this will going to make you obsolete one day.

Are you aware of the kind of changes you need to bring in? Many people don't feel the need to change. In fact they don't want to change. Most of us want system, friends, society, boss and everyone else to change but we hardly put any effort to change ourselves.

Change Your Habits and Thinking

We have many habits and actions which we have been doing for long without any logic or relevance. We never think why we are working like this. May be this is the way we have got accustomed to. We may have better ways to do things but we never explore new vistas. I remember a very interesting story which is apt to the topic being discussed:

Many years ago a saint was running a residential school (Ashram) where many students used to come for studies. The saint was having a cat, which was very notorious. Whenever there was pray in the morning the cat use to disturb the students. The saint got a big basket and started keeping it on the cat during the pray time and releasing her after the pray. Now their life is easy, they can pray without any disturbance. Few years later the saint died and senior most teacher of the school took his place as the head of the 'ashram'. The cat was still there and basket used to be kept on her during prayer. After few months cat also died and suddenly everything was stand still, prayer was stopped. A new cat was brought, kept on the prayer site, basket was kept on the new cat then only prayer began. The saint started keeping basket on the cat to resolve a problem but slowly and gradually it became a tradition. No one is putting brains why they are following this tradition. They are doing it simply because the head of the ashram used to do it.

We have many such habits and traditions in our life which we have been doing for years without any relevance to our life. Give it a thought and change such habits.

We don't want to change our way of thinking or working but yes we want different and extraordinary results, which is next to impossible. "Keeping on doing the same things which we have been doing for long and expecting different results is nothing but a sign of insanity".

Change Your Words to Change Your Life

When you change your words you will change your life. Think before you speak.

Make positive affirmations and create more happiness and success in your life. Try to use the following replacement words to create more self-confidence and to build self-esteem.

Replace the words "***I can't***" with "***I haven't yet.***"

Replace the words "***If I***" with "***When I.***"

Replace the words "***I will try***" with "***I will do.***"

Replace the words "***That's going to be a problem***" with "***That's going to be a challenge.***"

Replace the words "***I don't know***" with "***I will find out.***"

Replace the words "***What a failure***" with "***What a success --I learned something.***"

Practice using these replacement words until they become a natural automatic way of speaking and thinking, until they become a habit. You will be pleased with the results!

Change is Always Resisted

Nobody accepts changes easily not even our body. We are accustomed to work in a particular style and in spite of understanding the need to change we avoid it because we don't want to leave the comfort zone. The change causes discomfort and requires a lot of efforts. Those who are able to overcome the resistance are ahead of others because they become pioneer in implementing those changes.

You see, our bodies resist change, even positive change. It can't tell the difference between positive and negative changes.

Most of the times this is a good thing but still it resists. We want our bodies to work at cooling us off when the temperature is hot and to release insulin when our blood sugar rises, to begin the healing process when we get a cut. But when we want to lose weight or get in shape or dramatically increase our income, it's a big hindrance. George Leonard, author of Mastery, tells us that we have to negotiate with our resistance to change: "Negotiation is the ticket to successful long-term change in everything from increasing your running speed to transforming your organization".

One great way to negotiate with your resistance to change is to work WITH your body, even as it is resisting you, through your brainwaves.

Let me explain. Let's say you want to lose 10 Kg. of weight. You can send a message about this directly to your brain. In this way you bypass the conscious mind, which is resistant to change.

The subconscious is willing to call the shots for you, and help you accomplish the change that you want, if only you can get the right messages to it. We have already discussed this methodology in Chapter -3 under the title "Power of Subconscious".

Change or Get Perished

"It takes all the running you can do to keep yourself in the same place. If you want to go somewhere else, you must run at least twice as fast as that"

- Lewis Carroll."

Times have changed. It is a daringly different scenario today. Every second person is as good as the best, if not better. The ladder of success, which was once crowded at the bottom is now crowded at the TOP. Today's scenario demands - leaders, entrepreneurs and achievers aiming to go big, total resoluteness. It has to be amazed by your competence and a powerful passion. This awe-inspiring scenario - mandates you to get involved with newer approaches; ready to take on difficult situations; not get deterred by people who are a threat, and register a powerful impact by continuously performing better than your own previous.

There is not anymore a science, which can survive without new happenings. The creativity and innovation is required in every sphere of life viz. Education, business, management, thinking, Life-style. The pace at which the changes in these areas are taking place is constantly challenging the very survival of people. "*Kill the obsolete*" is driving people to find alternatives and outsmart the competition. Nothing can travel faster than the speed of light is now under threat from new interpretation and discoveries. Competition in the business arena has mandated change to be a routine process in order to assure customer acceptance. Wide product range, creative advertisement, attractive packaging, counting every inch of the shelf space, customer feedback all and many more add on to the list of the innovative ways of doing business in the present scenario.

Steve Jobs revolutionized the whole world through his innovations. He could only do it by thinking in different dimensions.

"Change your thoughts and you change your world."

- Norman Vincent Peale

Thomas Edison, The great American inventor, is yet another example of what can happen when we change the way we look at things. When Edison was 67 yrs old, his factory was virtually destroyed by a late-night fire and much of his life time's work went up in smoke. To make matter worst, the buildings were insured for only $238000, even though the damage exceeded $2 million!

The next morning Edison walked around his grounds surveying the smouldering ruins. Friends and family gathered around the old man, offering their regrets and condolences. Edison summoned all the visitors to his side and addressed their concerns with these:

"There is great value in disaster," he said evenly. Gesturing towards the gutted concrete buildings, Edison said, "Look, all of our mistakes have burned up. Thank God we can start a new now."

Just think, if Edison had taken the disaster as a disaster only, he could have used the fire as an excuse to give up, and the world would have missed out one of his greatest inventions. But he looked at the entire happening from a totally different angle. That is how a person's thought process determines his success.

For miraculously, only three weeks after the fire, Edison introduced an invention that would bring pleasure to hundreds of millions of people.....an invention that would go on to revolutionize the entertainment industry. That invention was the world's first phonogram!

It does not matter what the situation is, what counts ultimately is how you perceive it!

"The grand thing about the human mind is that it can turn its own tables and see meaninglessness as ultimate meaning"

- John Cage

While competition has been the driving force, creativity has been the hallmark of the changing scenario reflecting the most significant and appreciable innovations ever. Anything that was dropped off as not being logical an invention at some point of time, came back in a big way for consideration. Time proved that many written off concepts did have some meaning in the new context of their encashment.

The extent of creativity was amply demonstrated not only in the way new products were conceived or new innovations came in, but even in the way business took a new twist. The new business era is all about e-business fantasies. It is also influenced by the new wave of mergers; acquisitions; partnerships; alliances; takeovers or even getting the competitors to work together to be assured of the retention of their existing customers, and hence the need to work together to weaken a common opponent. Creative indeed!

What is Creativity?

Creativity is all about thoughts. Creativity is nothing but SEEING WHY AND ASKING WHY NOT. Thoughts that emerge out of a fertile mind that provide you with insights into the kind of problems you face and how to overcome them. You will see all fertile and creative minds will look ideas from this angle and consider various options before zeroing in the most appropriate one.

"Creativity is seeing what everybody has seen and thinking what nobody has thought."

Mere thoughts do not mean anything. Thoughts shall be directed towards a purpose that is relevant and need based. There are people who keep on dreaming and never wake up. The purposeful and result oriented persons keep dreaming with their eyes open. Applied creativity is what we should be concerned about than mere conceiving of ideas.

In 1957, a group of 24 scientists were asked to predict what they thought the world would be like in 20 years. These scientists represented different fields and came from different parts of the world. Among their predictions were, that in 1977 individual diets would include meat and vegetables which would be stored in cupboards-that is no refrigerators would be needed, automobiles would be of automatic control models and the grass would grow at a certain height only and would not grow further so that it would never need mowing.

These predictions were all based on future 20 years away, but less than 15 months later, a large chemical products company had a display board in their research centre with packages of meat and vegetables that had been there for six months at room temperature because they had been irradiated with gamma rays. General Motors introduced their new experimental car that can be guided automatically. In an electronic highway which was then being tested.

That is what Albert Einstein, the most creative man the world has never seen told, **"Whatever one man is capable of conceiving, the other man will be able to achieve."** Creativity deals with conceiving of ideas.

The Magic of Creativity

If a "fried chicken" recipe would have been perceived as just a recipe by a retired soldier called Colonel Sanders, Kentucky Fried Chicken would not have been born. An empire was created based on this recipe. Or the escaping steam by James Watt....Or the apple which fell on the head....

The Four C's

The world of today, as never before, is on the fast track – not just in fleeting seconds, but all the 24 hours, all days. As Rich Meiss said, ***"Today, with increasing demands on people and organizations, our world is characterized by four C's.***

"The world is moving so fast often somebody who says something can't be done is proved wrong by somebody already doing it."

- Narayan Murthy

Competition: Both nationally and internationally more and more companies are competing for the same amount of business. More small businesses are starting up, more large companies are diversifying into other areas, and more international companies are competing to acquire a larger share of the market.

Complexity: Even though, we seem to be more sophisticated and aware, it seems as if there is more to learn. And the answers to the questions seem harder to get. As someone said, "I thought I know all the answers, until I realized that someone was playing with the questions."

Change: Knowledge and information has exploded. One analyst estimated the following:

- Knowledge doubled between 0-1700 A.D.
- Knowledge doubled again between 1700-1900.
- Knowledge doubled again between 1900-1950.
- Knowledge doubled again between 1950-1960.
- Today, in almost all fields, knowledge is doubling every year. And talking about new technology and computers.... You can never say.... May be knowledge doubles every day!

How to Start Innovating

Be open to new ideas. Keep looking for new knowledge and learning, stay curious and keep riding your bicycle to update yourself on consistent basis. Look for better ways to do the same thing.

At Toyota, the starting-point is the suggestion-box system. All employees are invited to put forward suggestions for improvements. People are rewarded if their suggestions are adopted. This is a simple but effective way of letting everyone know that their ideas are welcomed and providing a way in which they can contribute.

The important thing about innovation is that it invariably has a systems knock-on effect. If you change something in one job, or one task, or one area then it will have an impact on other jobs, tasks, and areas. That is why teamwork and a language for the sharing of team innovations, is crucial.

The Innovation Process

It's not simply a matter of saying, "Tomorrow morning I will spend some time innovating". It is more of a process, and needs to be built into the very fabric of the team. The team leader of a well-known design group in Europe said, "In our team we encourage people to ask, "Why are we doing things this way?" Our innovations have come about by people analyzing how tasks are carried out in the home and then asking why we cannot make something to assist.

"A dream is your creative vision for your life in the future. It's what you would like life to become."

- Denis Waitley

Creativity is the sole way to reach the new and a better way to survive, succeed and outshine in this world. The first step to fulfil your dream is to create change. Change is inevitable. Now it is up to you whether to follow the change or to lead the change. If you fail to move with the world's pace you are out of the race. It's not only to be in the race that change is must. In order to lead one has to be a trendsetter. Ultimately that is what determines the altitude of your success in life.

7

The Success Highway

I have seen people struggling with life and living in miserable conditions, I have seen people not trying hard and taking excuses of self fulfilling prophecies, I have seen people falling from top to bottom and I have also seen people and organization leaving their success track. Now there are different set of people and organization too. There are people who live in miserable conditions but never accept that as a destiny and strive hard, to come out of it and they do. There are such people also who never felt contended with what they have achieved instead they are tempted towards "What is still to be attained?", It's not material for them that they are on the top right now but they perceive, plan and work for staying on the top in future also.

That's why somebody has rightly said "Success is a journey not a destination". If someone says that I have attained success and stop trying further, the decline begins. Those who are more successful are more vulnerable. Success actually results in complacency, inefficiency, arrogance and overconfidence. They stop trying new things, they stop expanding and they fail to upgrade themselves as per the current scenario. Finally they lose their position and start declining. That's why renowned management guru and prolific writer 'Robin Sharma' says "Nothing fails like Success". I have seen plenty of such persons, business groups and companies in my close vicinity, falling flat when they were right on top.

Success: An Ongoing Process

To me, success is the ongoing process of striving to become better than the previous state. It is the opportunity to continually grow emotionally, socially, spiritually, intellectually, and financially while contributing in some positive ways. The road to success is always busy and needs continuous improvement. It is a progressive course which ends nowhere.

People who have attained excellence follow a consistent path to success. Renowned writer from U.S. Anthony Robins calls it the **"Ultimate Success Formula"**. The first step to this formula is to know your outcome, that is, to define precisely what you want. The second step is to take action otherwise your desires will always be dreams. You must take the types of actions you believe will create the greatest probability of producing the result you desire.

Here is one of the best success stories, which has inspired millions on this earth.

*You would have heard of KFC i.e. "**Kentucky Fried Chicken**". Do you know how Col. Saunders built the empire that made him a millionaire and changed the eating habits of a nation? When he started, he was nothing but a retired military man willing to start a small business having a fried-chicken recipe learned from his mother. He had owned a little restaurant that was going broke because the main highway had been routed elsewhere. When he got his first pension cheque he decided to sell the chicken recipe. His first idea was to sell the recipe to restaurant owners and have them give him a percentage of the proceeds. He was rejected 1009* *times and then something miraculous happened. Someone said "Yes." The colonel was in business. Today KFC has thousands of restaurants across the globe and his family is still getting royalty of millions of dollars.*

How many of you have a recipe or an idea? How many of you have the physical power and passion what that old man had? Col. Sanders made a fortune because he had the ability to take daring and quick action. He had the inherent power necessary to produce the results he desired most about. He had the ability to hear word "no" a thousand times and still charged up after every rejection and got excited about his action.

He would have stopped after opening up few restaurants in the city itself. That was enough for him to spend the life lavishly but he didn't. He strived for more, he was running on the success highway and that's what helped him building a global, unique and the most successful organization.

"To laugh often and much; to win the respect of intelligent people and the affection of children; to earn the appreciation of honest critics and endure the betrayal of false friends; to appreciate beauty, to find the best in others; to leave the world a bit better, whether by a healthy child, a garden patch or a redeemed social condition; to know even one life has breathed easier because you have lived. This is to have succeeded."

- Ralph Waldo Emerson

The Success Mantras

The success highway is based on certain natural principles. You may be a student, an entrepreneur, an executive in a company, a social worker, a politician or even a house wife.

You need to tread the path with same principles. The course of action is almost similar though the modus operandi may be different.

1. **The Rock Solid Belief:**

   Every life management, spiritual and religious book in the universe tells about Self-belief. People usually ask me "what's that ingredient, which differentiates successful people from those who failed?" My reply is same every time and that's BELIEF. I believe in a famous saying "A man is what he believes." So, the belief about what you are, the belief about where you can reach and what you could be makes all the difference. There are billions of people on the earth who never believe what they have and what they can do, they shrink their limits and never try to break the shackles. Before you do anything you need to have a rock solid belief which is not shakable in the worst of the circumstances.

2. **Power up your Passion:**

   What's passion? Which drives you to do toughest of the things with smile on your face and sparkle in your eyes, Which makes you feel challenged and Which infuses the competitive spirit. You should have an obsession for what you are striving for and this obsession does never let you feel tired or disheartened. If you have that passion the small debacles on the way should energize you rather than disappointing. It gives you the fuel that certainly powers your success wagon and producing the desired results. You think of any successful business person, a sportsman, a leader, an artist the only common thing you will discover in them is the passion they had for their object.

You need to discover the passion and power it up don't let it get fad.

3. **A Full Proof Plan:**

   If you fail to plan you certainly plan your failures. A plan is a process of organizing resources. It's a process where we predict everything well in advance and have pre planned tool for every situation.

   When the famous Hollywood film maker Steven Spielberg who is known for the film "Jurassic Park" all over the world, decided to become a film-maker, he chalked out a course that would enable him to attain what he dreamt. Every industrialist, student, artist, leader knows it's not enough to have resources to succeed. The effective utilization is a must. You can open a door by breaking it down or you can find the key that opens it intact.

4. **A Crystal Clear Value System:**

   Values play an important role in our decision making process. That's what tells us what is right and what is wrong. They are the judgments we make about what makes life worth living. Many people do not have a clear idea of what is important to them. Often people do things those afterwards make them unhappy with themselves, simply because they were not clear in their heads. I will advise you to have a very-very clear value system. Once you have this you may not face the situation which confuses you to take an apt decision.

5. **An Ocean of Energy:**

   Great success is inseparable from the physical, mental, intellectual, and spiritual energy that allows us to make the most of what we have. Many a time we fail to give attention to our physical needs and maintenance. Afterwards, even you are willing to do something but lack of physical energy forces you to withdraw. Sometime you are fit and fine physically but that's not supported by your unenergetic mind. The message is very clear if want to have an ongoing and consistent speed on the success highway you need to emerge as an ocean of energy by putting constant efforts on daily basis by giving appropriate input to your mind, body and soul.

I want you to read the speech given by renowned author Chetan Bhagat at Symbiosis.

"Don't just have career or academic goals. Set goals to give you a balanced and successful life. I used the word 'balanced' before 'successful'. Balanced means ensuring your health, relationships and mental peace are all in good order. There is no point of getting a promotion on the day of your break up. There is no fun driving a car if your back hurts. Shopping is not enjoyable if your mind is full of tensions. Life is one of those races in nursery school where you have to run with a marble in a spoon kept in your mouth. If the marble falls, there is no point coming first. Same is with life where health and relationships are like marbles. Your striving is only worth it if there is harmony in your life. Else you may achieve the success but this spark, this excitement will start to die and will hinder in upcoming success."

6. **Rapport Building Skill:**

We live in people word and if we want to be successful we need to know how we should work with them, how we can make them happy and how fast we can make relationship. Almost all successful people have in common an extraordinary ability to bond with others, the ability to connect with and develop rapport with people from a variety of backgrounds and beliefs. This is what that makes you a versatile person in all groups. You are compatible to everyone so what if those groups are different from each other.

7. **Expertise in Communication:**

   You know we have two types of communication one which we have internally with ourselves and other which we have with the outer world. The way we communicate with others and the way we communicate with ourselves ultimately determine the quality of our lives. People who succeed in life are those who have learned how to take any challenge that life gives them and communicate that experience to themselves in a way that causes them to successfully change things. There are people who use the world "problem" to a situation and others may call it an opportunity or a challenge.

"The words you use determine the way you feel. The language you choose shapes the way you perceive reality. Your vocabulary drives meaning in your life."

- Robin Sharma

The Journey Starts with Belief

"Beliefs are like commanders of the brain. Belief delivers a direct command to your nervous system. When you believe something is true, you literally go into the state of its being true. Handled effectively, beliefs can be the most powerful forces for creating best in your life."

- Anthony Robins

Norman cousin was told by doctors that because of terminal disease he has he can't survive for more than six months. He decided not to stay in the hospital and returned home. He started living life in his own style without taking stress about his life but a belief was inside him which constantly iterated that he is going to be survived. His belief led him to live for several years without any medical treatment. He learned the power of belief in eradicating his disease.

One fabulous study relating to a group of patient having bleeding ulcer: The group was divided in to two sub groups. Patients in the one group were told that they are being given a new drug that will absolutely produce relief. Those in the second group were told they were being given an experimental drug, but that very little was known about its effects. Seventy percent of those in the first group experienced significant relief from their ulcers. Only 25% of second group had a similar result. The astonishing fact of the study is in both the groups patients received a drug with no medical properties at all. The only difference was the belief system they adopted.

How Belief Gets Shaped?

- Environment is the first source of belief. The environment you stay has the direct bearing over your belief system.
- Each one of us has certain moments or events in our lives which can never be forgotten. Similarly the experience, which we had in those moments also remain permanently in our mind. These are the experiences that shape up our belief which may eventually change our whole life.
- The knowledge is such a powerful tool which can create limitless boundaries for you. Don't worry if you have life with a limited span, if you can read

about the achievements of others, you can inculcate the beliefs that will enable you to succeed.

- The sure shot solution to create a belief that you can do something is to do it once. If it is clicked once, its indeed very easy to have the belief of doing things in the similar fashion.
- Now it's very important and powerful idea I am sharing with you. I wrote that your past experiences will have bearing on your belief system because it's stored permanently inside your mind. Same way whatever you imagine about future, whatever you visualize will also be stored in the same manner. If you have fear in public speaking, you should start visualizing that you are speaking in front of thousands of people and at the end of the speech you are getting a standing ovation. The words like "Wonderful, Fantastic, Superb, amazing, are coming from audiences". Once you start the habit of imagining opposite to your fears very soon you will develop that belief of converting those visualizations into reality.

Renowned Hollywood star Jim Carrey wanted to be a great actor and aspired to earn handsome money. One day he made a cheque in his own name for $ 1million and got it framed, he used to have a look over it every day. The day came when he got the same for a Hollywood film "Mask".

There is another story of a student who incidentally slept during the class. When he woke up at the end of the class he saw a problem written on the black board, he copied that in his note book. He thought that this is home work for the day. He got back to home and tried whole night but could not solve the problem. He kept on trying for few more days and finally he could solve the same and showed it to the teacher. The teacher was shocked. While writing this problem on the black board teacher told students that this problem is unsolvable. But since he didn't hear that and his mind entered into limitless zone of trying. Other students did not try for it because the words of the teacher limited their virtual ability.

Almost similar things happen to all of us plenty of times in our life. During the course of life we limit our abilities without giving it a try. Those who dare to come out of their box and think without prejudice produce altogether different results. Choice is yours!!!

Choice is Yours!!!

The world we live in is the world we choose to live in, whether consciously or unconsciously. If we choose bliss, that's what we get. If we choose misery, we get that too.

Results or Failures

Don't name an event a failure when you don't get the expected result. There are no failures in life only results. Those who believe in failures can't come out of the mediocrity. We may have a culture in our surroundings where getting inferior results are named as failures. If you don't get what you expect, no need to feel disappointment. Just go and work on the improvement of the previous result you will have better one next time.

The story of Abraham Lincoln is witness of it: He failed in business at age 21, was defeated in a legislative election at age 22, failed again in business at age 24, Overcame the death of his sweetheart at age 26, Had a nervous breakdown at age 27, Lost a congressional election at age 34 and again at 36, Lost a senatorial election at age 45, Failed in an effort to become vice-president at age 47, Lost a senatorial election at age 49, Was finally elected president of the United States at age 52.

If we have something called failure in our mind dictionary we start giving infectious dose to our mind which along with stores negative feelings and emotions. The process affects our health, thought process and our action too.

One of my favorite writers Dr. Robert Schuller says, "What would you attempt to do if you knew you could not fail?" Think about it then answer. If you really believed you could not fail, you might take a whole new set of actions and produce remarkable results.

Be Responsible for Your Action

You have to learn accepting responsibility. You have to have a firm belief that you have the power to create your own world. You are not going to blame anyone for any result. The sayings like "I am responsible for it", "I will see it", "I will control it", "I will produce the results", are going to help taking your own responsibility religiously.

Start the Day Like a New Chapter of Your Life

We spend most of our life thinking for others, working for others and worrying for silly matters. But start doing something different from today itself. Keep one hour every day exclusively for yourself, preferably in the morning. During this slot you can meditate, read something good, listen to soothing music and give a thought to your day ahead. This will certainly help you starting your day with lots of energy and positive thoughts which will ultimately enhance your personal effectiveness in every field.

Learn to Prioritize

You must have heard of the rule called 80:20. It says that 80% of your time should go to 20% significant part of your life and the balance 20% should go to the rest 80% things. Why don't we achieve what we dream because we hardly give time to most important activities of our life. Majority of people are badly occupied with unimportant things at the cost of critical matters. You learn to prioritize things as per 80:20 rule on daily basis and see the change within a month.

Focus on the Purpose

Never deviate from your very purpose of life. Keep your Mind, Body and Soul aligned to the purpose. Your every day, every hour and every minute should contribute something towards the attainment of your personal, professional, social or family objectives.

Enhance Your Will-Power

Your will power is a source of energy which never let you down in sad times. When you are confronted with the adverse situations, it gives you encouragement to not to give up and stay there with full enthusiasm and courage. You should put all your endeavors to enhance your will power.

Be Focused

Start living in present and keep focused on one thing at a time. Don't think of anything else while you are working on one project. I know its very difficult indeed to follow this discipline but once you start trying this consciously very soon you will develop the habit.

Stretch Little More

Start stretching yourself viz. If you are doing sit ups try to do two more. I know it will cause some pain. When T.V.

is tempting you to watch, just hold on for few minutes. If you are feeling like sleeping just postpone it by few minutes try to concentrate in the book you are reading. By this you will learn keeping patience which will directly contribute to your will power enhancement.

Substitute Your Negative Thoughts

Start learning substitution of negatives. An ordinary human being conceives thousands of negative thoughts in 24 hours. The best way to get rid of this is whenever you conceive a negative thought just substitute it with the positive one. Gradually you will become habitual of generating positive thoughts in abundance.

Add Value Everyday

At the end of the day, just give it a thought, what's your value addition for the day. Do something every day which causes improvement in you, your knowledge & experience. A little value which you add on a daily basis will become significant in few months.

Develop the Adventurous Spirit

By developing adventurous spirit you can revive, rekindle or develop a sense of a being a kid. I am not asking you to be kid. But the adventurous feel a kid has we lose it over the years. Consequently we forget the joy of challenges and thrills. At least once or twice in month you indulge yourself in an activity which makes you feel thrilled. If you can manage spare some time to play with kids, you will develop this spirit.

Find a Mentor

Learning from others experience is something which not only saves your time but also keeps you ahead from others. If you can find a person whom you can model as a mentor then your progress will be far better, your decision making process becomes faster. Find such a person who has experience and skill of guiding people.

Emerge as a Prolific Thinker

Keep yourself well-informed about current events, the latest books and prevailing trends, you will certainly become a prolific thinker. Many great performers have a habit of reading five or six news papers a day. You don't have to read every story of every paper. Know what to focus on, what to skip and what to take out for repetitive reading. Knowledge is powerful tool through which you can have edge over others. Whether you are an entrepreneur, a corporate leader or someone leading a family or simply a student you can drastically change your life and the lives of those around you with a single idea. Just think of people like Thomas Edison, 'Dhirubhai Ambani' and other great legends.

Set Your Worries to Fire

You can control your thought process effectively through visualization technique. If something is bothering you consistently and not letting you work just put your worries on a piece paper and set it to fire. After sometime you will see that your worries have dissipated into flames. This is a mind control device used by many successful persons including players and artists.

Inculcate the Habit of Reading

Put yourself into the great habit of reading something positive and inspirational on regular basis. I know one of my Friend Dr. Suresh Goyal who always keeps a book with him, wherever he gets couple of minutes he starts reading the book. Because of him I could inculcate the reading habit and today I have a collection of more than 2000 books at my home. These books are best companion of ours. I read somewhere that the Former U.S. President Bill Clinton read more than 300 books when he was at Oxford University. Read few pages of an inspirational book before you go to sleep and do the same at the day beginning. The changes you will notice will be mind blowing.

Keep the Grooming Process On

I am very much impressed with a quote ***"The quality doesn't have a finish line."*** This prompts me to add value to my personality every day. We must have one goal across the life i.e. to develop a dynamic and powerful personality. A study says that an ordinary human being is able to explore 10-20% of his hidden capabilities. Each one of us has immense potential and infinite possibilities to explore but we never try anything on regular basis. Start reading something good on daily basis, Join some part time classes to learn new skills, get into the habit of socializing.

Find Time to Relax

Relaxing never means lying down on the bed and killing the time instead get into the habit of going for mental vacations. This indeed works as an energizer and refuels you for upcoming week or month. The results will be significant once you try it for six months.

Rewind the Favourite Song

What we do when we listen to our most favourite song, we like to listen it repetitively. My father keeps telling me that look for what you want you will certainly get it. We must keep our targets and ambitions in front of our eyes. Repeat your goals and targets five ten times a day and visualize them as if you have attained them. It's truly said "If someone is miser in dreaming, God will be miser in giving". Dream big, dream high and visualize them till the moment you don't attain them.

Some men see things as they are and say 'why?' I dream of things that never were and say 'why not?'"

- George Bernard Shaw

Walk an Extra Mile

Just imagine one situation when you go for a vacation and return back to home. The start of journey looks very interesting but the last hour of the journey looks very boring and non-tolerable. When we do something we are full of energy and power at the beginning but what about the final lap. We really feel tired and wish to finish the task some-how. The energy level gets down to its bottom. Then, how can we get desired results. We should push ourselves little further every time when we accomplish something with the same level of energy and diligence. We need to be mentally tougher towards end just like marathon runners who keep some energy saved for the last lap and put their best at that time. This will help you building your strength and character on a higher side. If you do exercise on daily basis and your capacity is 14 sit ups, then try to stretch it to 16 and increase it day by day. You should apply this method to other areas too.

Stay Optimistic

All those who have done something exceptional in their lives and attained significant results have at least learned one thing i.e. the habit of staying positive and optimistic. Without this life loses its glamour and adversities appear at every footstep of your path. This is one of the best energy savers, which keeps you full of energy even though you are physically exhausted.

Convert Unpleasant Task into Pleasant One

During the course of our life we develop our liking and disliking for doing something or the other. Now if you want a successful and balanced life you need to develop liking for unpleasant tasks too. Do couple of things everyday which generally you don't feel like doing. This will not only help you gaining more personal power and productivity but will also help you building strength.

Do What You Love

I haven't seen anybody achieving great success by doing what he or she hates. One of the keys to become more effective and successful is to choose what you are passionate about. Thomas Edison was once questioned that how could, he work so much to have more than 1000 inventions to his credit, his reply was terrific. He told "I didn't work for a single day in my life, I just had fun and the results are in front of you." Either choose what you love to do or else develop the affinity for what you are already doing you will never have to worry about the results. *Mark Twain said, "**The secret of success is making your vocation your vacation.**"*

And Finally, Understand Only What's Important

"It's not necessary to understand everything to be able to use everything"

– Anthony Robins

Successful people know how to use what's essential without feeling a need to get bogged down in every detail of it. They are especially good at making distinctions between what is necessary for them to understand and what is not.

8

Passion, The Elixir

DREAMS

"Dreamt by all
desired by many
converted into goals by some
A handful get passionate

And

Those handful are
Called as achievers"

Life is a miracle-if you call it a failure it fails, you call it a success it becomes a paradigm for the rest of the world. It's not only about thinking, or dreaming of success, but it is actually the process of living success, living every moment of your life to make it a success!!

Mentally Tough People – Willingness To Live

A Person called W. Mitchell was driving the vehicle at almost 90 Km. an hour speed when his concentration got deviated for a fraction of second looking at road side and when he looked to his front he had a second to respond. A big size truck came to unexpected stop. Instantly, in an effort to save his life, he laid his motorcycle down into a sickening skid that seemed to last forever. In agonizingly slow motion, he slid beneath the truck. The petrol cap popped off his motorcycle, and the worst occurred: fuel spilled out and ignited.

His next moment of consciousness is the experience of waking up in a hospital bed in searing pain, unable to move, fearing to breathe. Almost 75% of his body is covered by terrible third degree burns. Still, he refuses to give up. He struggles back to life and resumes a business career, only to suffer another staggering blow: an airplane crash that leaves him paralyzed, from the waist down, for life. This person is one of the most vital, strong and successful people and still living in USA. Since his terrible motorcycle accident, he has known more success and joy than most people know in a lifetime.

The obsession to live does not need 'physical strength' to get through, it requires a strong Will Power- an unfailing consistent vigor to win over the hardships and live our dreams to the fullest. Whether you are physically fit or not? as long as you can dream you can also shape your dreams into reality.

There is one more such legend called 'Pete Strudwick'. He was born with no hands and no feet, he became a marathon runner who had run for more than 25000 miles. He was able to finish the run of Pike's Peak, the most difficult marathon in the world, even though he has no hands and no feet! How do these people, could overcome such adverse & horrifying situations and turned their life from disaster to triumph? Why do some people take any experience and make it work for them, while others take any experience and make it work against them?

Life is all about, how you react towards different situations. Taking responsibility of your own action and developing an attitude of not giving up in toughest of the situation. It is just the way you communicate to your mind and what instructions you give in such situations make the huge difference. In painful situations feeling helpless and frustrated is one option and showing strength, giving signals to your mind of overcoming the adverse situation is another. Let me be clear, if you give messages to your mind that in spite of the critical problems in your life you will be able to resume your normal life very soon, your mind and body will start responding to it positively.

Every person once in life time faces a very tough challenge and a real exam of person's character takes place. Amidst such situation one may feel that god is unfair to him and start losing the faith and patience. Some extra ordinary people prove themselves, tougher than the situation and emerge as a more successful and better individual while majority of people allow the situation to rule over them and that ruins their life. Choice is absolutely yours. The way you perceive the situation and the way you respond to the problems shape your destiny.

Remember Attitude Determines Your Altitutde

It is your positive attitude that plays a crucial role in growing high despite all odds. Your optimistic approach, enthusiastic words and commitment towards your future plans help you face the challenges and go beyond your limits. Every situation, every hurdle and every problem has a brighter side too. You need to look out for that positive side of the situation and move ahead. This is what exactly keeps the spirit on!!

KEEP THE SPIRIT ON......

When everything starts going wrong..... Be positive!
When your business goes down ...... Be positive!
When yours dear and near ones leave your hand ..... Be positive!

When all your possessions start getting deteriorated.....
Be positive!
When the world no more believes in you..... Be Positive!
Keep the spirit ON until Desirous Happens!
Keep the spirit ON until Desirous Happens!!!

The Bumpy Road of Your Life Make You More Strong

A farmer used to grow potatoes but never took pains of grading them but still he used to earn more than other growers. Ultimately one of his envious neighbours asked the secret of his earning more. He said "Very easy". "I simply put these potatoes in a van and follow the worst of the road to city". After the journey is over, small potatoes go down. The mediocre size potatoes remain in between and the big size potatoes come on the top.

The same rule is well valid in our lives. Those who keep themselves firm during the bad roads of life always reach to the top. Whatever difficulties come on your way, they are new to your life but if we look at it from an observer's view the difficulties are nothing new under the sun. When it is the same set of difficulties that keeps on moving from one person to another, then why does the ultimate outcome of these difficulties vary from each one of us? It is just the way we perceive things. It all depends on how much we explore ourselves. There is a powerhouse with immense potential in each one of us. Success ultimately depends on the extent to which we make use of that inner power. We need to put in our best of efforts consistently. It is this consistent effort to explore our self that enhances our mental toughness.

While going through the tough times of life, hardships would be in the severest state, challenging our mental toughness, questioning our perseverance and almost bringing our faith level to zero. It is at this peak moment that our belief support system comes into play.

"Self belief is the most wonderful and miraculous power. It never leaves you. Whenever it gets the savour of being unsuccessful we leave it."

Passion to its Peak

The first person who conquered the Mount Everest, Sir Edmond Hillary once went for mountaineering with his schoolmates. It was first time when he went for mountaineering. He was too excited when he got back. He asked his teacher, "Teacher tell me, which is the highest peak on the earth?" Teacher replied, "It's Mt. Everest but why did you ask"? The boy replied, "Nothing special, I would love to go there once in my life". The teacher was stunned with the response of the child but left the conversation then and there.

When the boy grew up, he went to that mighty mission with few of his colleagues. It was tough and cruel, half the way few of them fell sick and their resources got finished, hardly anything to eat. They decided to return back and come again with better preparation. Edmond was very upset with his unsuccessful efforts. One of his excited friends organized a party to felicitate Sir Edmond Hillary. After some dignitaries spoke on the mighty challenges Hillary took and how he made it mission of his life, the convener called Sir Edmond on the dais to speak about his experiences. He was feeling too shy to speak on a mission that was failed but had no choice but to speak. He went on stage holding mike in his hands and looking at the picture of Mount Everest at the Backdrop. He didn't look at the audiences, looking at the picture of Mt. Everest uttered few lines and got back to his seat. He spoke "Mount Everest you have defeated me, but don't worry I will come again. I know you can't grow bigger than what you are but my preparation, determination and zeal to conquer will be far better than what you have seen earlier."

And we know he made the history later by conquering the Mt. Everest and became the first person to do that. Until he did that, he had only one mission, one thought and one passion to conquer the Mt. Everest. Throughout the day and the whole night he had only one thought to perceive and one target to achieve. In spite of his failure in first attempt he didn't get frustrated, rather he became more strong and firm. That response of him to the situation made him achieving that mighty mission. His preparedness, continuous efforts and firm determination towards the mission made him successful and known to the whole world.

Such obsession in life drives you beyond your own potential and spurs in you a fountain of positive mental energy. A focused approach, a goal-oriented movement in life never makes you feel low. Passion is a strong inner striving for a positive thing, for a good outcome. Your inner power is so competent that if you guide it in the right direction it can do miracles, thus making the impossible possible. When you become a passionate mover in life, you enjoy every moment of your life, and it is actually then that you make your life worth living. It is your 'passion' that makes every single second of your life contributes in making your dream, a reality.

When Passion Turns into Obsession

The courage and will of this man is one of those rare real life incidents which will continue to inspire mankind for ages to come. This simple man from a village in Gaya district of Bihar (India) had the fortitude and conviction to move mountain and he made it happen by his sheer perseverance and faith in his efforts to move the mountain. He is an inspiration for many and just when you feel chips are down and the road ahead seems tough, put yourself in his shoes and imagine the courage it took to move a mountain.

Yes, this man literally moved a mountain! Alone, just by his sheer will and perseverance.

In 1960 landless labourer Dashrath Manjhi got hold of a chisel and a hammer and decided to change the face of his village nestled in the rocky hills of Gaya. He almost tore open a 300-feet-high hill to create a one-km passage. Instead of endlessly waiting for the apathetic administration to do something for those formidable hills that virtually cut his village off from civilization, He, then in his early 20s, took up a chisel and hammered at the rocks for 22 years.

It all started from Manjhi's love for his wife. For, when she slipped off the rocks while getting food for him as he worked in a field beyond the hill and broke her ankle, it became a burning passion to tame the formidable hills. And he completed this Herculean task — creating a short-cut which reduced a long and hard journey from his village Gahlor Ghati to Wazirganj to a walkable distance. At that time people called him mad. They ridiculed him. Even his wife and parents were against this "adventure," especially when he sold his goats to buy a chisel, a hammer and rope.

But, by then, Manjhi was a determined man. He shifted his hut close to the hill so he could work all day and night, chipping away, little by little. Many times he did not even bother to eat. With most of the cultivable land and shops across the hill, villagers had to cross it many times a day, braving dangers. It was after 10 years that people began to notice a change in the shape of the hill. Instead of a defiant rock face, the hill seemed to have a depression in the middle. Climbing it became a little easier. All those who had called him mad began to quietly watch him work. Some even chipped in.

Then in 1982, twenty-two years after he had actually started, that day came when Manjhi walked through a clear flat passage — about 16-feet wide — to the other side of the hill. But his victory was tinged with sadness. His wife, who inspired him to take on this task, was not by his side. She had died of illness. They could not take her to a hospital on time.

But, the villagers were there to celebrate with him. They got him sweets, fruits and all that they could afford. The young generation in that area had grown up hearing stories of the man who wanted to move a mountain. Now that dream was the reality and a boon for them.

This formidable task, single handed performed by Dashrath Manjhi, resulted into a 1.5 kilometre long road through the Gahlore Mountain thus reducing the distance to cross the mountain from a gruelling 50 kilometre to a much-easier 8 kilometre.

This hand-carved passage through the hill still remains the only sustainable change his village has ever chanced upon.

He died at the age of 78 battling with prolonged cancer but his deeds and herculean accomplishment has already written with golden words in the history. One man made the difference. He proved impossible word to be wrong. He made it his passion which turned into obsession despite all odds.

I am repeating myself, "Life throws many challenges. It's up to you how you respond to those challenges. Your courage and passion can turn those challenges into opportunities. Amidst all problems, adversities and challenges your passion makes you stay in battle, fight with odds and help you in emerging as a champion. Instead of cursing your life or luck you should believe in your capabilities and conviction and work hard towards a focused goal with determination and zeal".

Chase Your Dreams with Passion

When I dreamt of having rosy situation,
Life gave me adverse challenges.

When I dreamt of having great mind,
Life gave me difficult puzzles to solve.

When I dreamt of having pleasures,
Life made me meet many sad people.

When I dreamt of having money and luxuries,
Life gave me all hardships and miseries.
When I dreamt of having golden opportunities,
Life gave me heavy responsibilities.

When I dreamt of having peace in life,
Life showed me the people who need help.

Life didn't give me what I dreamt of,
But it made me strong enough, To Chase those dreams
with passion.
(Composed by Pritam Kumar Goswami)

What you need is already there within you but what all you can make out of it, depends solely on you! God has already provided us with all that is needed to fulfil our dreams. It's the need of the hour to realize the power potential within ourselves and make its optimum utilization in our valuable lives.

Optimizing the Power

- Learn to believe in yourself. Self belief is the first step to realize your hidden potential. If you don't believe in yourself you cannot believe anybody. But if you trust your inner self, then you may use that inner power to reach to your destination.
- Forget your past injuries and bad experiences that make you feel weak and disappointed. Focus on future and keep moving forward with positive and optimistic mindset, you will feel more powerful.
- Almost two-thousand-five-hundred years ago Lao Tzu, a famous Chinese philosopher, said that the biggest problem in the world was that individuals experienced themselves as powerless. This statement is still valid and many people feel themselves incompetent because they are not able to come out of their painful past. You must delete the negative thoughts that make you feel inferior, rather search out for the more complete, fulfilled and enriched image of self! Such a visualization of self will move you from powerless to powerful!
- Create a vocabulary of a successful, positive, inspiring individual. Your words reaffirm your thoughts in your mind. So the more the positive words you give to yourself the more the positive thoughts get stronger in your mind.

- Be passionate in your speech and let your enthusiasm be evident through words you speak. There should be a consistent flow of endless energy in you. And the same can be expressed by your vocal exposure. Such an approach not only keeps you energetic, but it makes the environment more conducive. It fills the environment around you with positive vibes.
- The energy of the words that you speak is a powerful force that is creative. Thus to be great have a great vocabulary!

PROBLEM ☹ ???... NO PROBLEM ☺

There would be times, when your passion would be questioned or ridiculed by your own people, when your own positivity would reach a low, when you start seeing scary obstacles ahead and you start feeling that going further is really becoming tough. It is at this moment where the flame of hope gets dim but the inner spark comes into play. It becomes the source of survival. It is in the light of the inner spark that makes the problem become 'no problem' for us.

Fueling the Spark Within

- **Problems are integral part of life:**

  Successful people have more and bigger problems but we think that they are free of problems. Everybody thinks that his or her problems are bigger than others i.e. grass of other side always looks green. Nobody is exempted from problems; Big businessman has big problems, problem-less life is a wrong notion or imagination. Therefore, take problems take as an integral part of your life and tackle them as you face other routine things. If you stop getting challenges in your life you need to check your direction.

- **Problems are not everlasting:**

  In life we confront with many good or bad situations. It has both shinier and darker sides. All problems have expiry date. Problems don't last long, but our determination and will power makes us come out of them. We see sun rise after every thunder. Winter always leads to spring. Thus all adverse situations & difficult times will pass by.

- **Problem have something to offer:**

  Problems are like two sides of a coin. One side it's a problem other way round it's an opportunity. We need to take it as an opportunity. If we do so our focus is diverted from problem towards the opportunity and we start putting our positive efforts for the cause forgetting the darker side.

- **Problems will refine you:**

  Whenever we pass through a problematic situation, we go through a process of refinement. We get more matured and experienced and become more sustainable for upcoming challenges. Just have a look over background of great legends in the world. You will find that existence of problems in their life played critical role to their success. If life gives you more problems, feel happy, it is giving you better chances of going up and growing.

  Therefore, the difficulties and hard times you pass through would bring a tangible improvement in you. This continuous improvement helps you attaining your long cherished dream and also in growing into a better person each time.

- **Control your reaction to the problem:**

  Problems are bound to occur in your life, you may not control them. What you can control is your reaction to the same. If you don't put in your positive energy, the instinct to fight goes down. If you take it sportingly and seriously work to combat with it you will get more energy and conviction to get out of the problem.

  One of the pilots in UK Air Force lost his both limbs in a crash and was living on artificial limbs. During second world-war, the country needed more pilots urgently, this ex-pilot offered himself to serve the country, he was refused on physical grounds but he didn't give up. Finally he was given chance to jump into the battle. In spite of huge deficiency he exhibited amazing character, fought with lots of courage. He was caught by German soldiers thrice and he was able to escape every time.

  Never ever think of quitting under difficult circumstances. Stay in the battle, have faith on your abilities and keep working towards your goals and I tell you, you yourself will force your problems to quit.

Cheer up Success!

The Things that make you what you are
Are worthy now of mention
You move ahead with your plans
With ambition, eagerness and dedication

The Voice of "I CAN & I WILL"
Should be intermingled with great determination
You ambitiously reach your goals,
Leaving behind a direction.

When days just seem like gloom and doom
Puzzled at life's station.

Be energetic and cheerful
To attain your destination
Move ahead with faith & love and
Be a star of god's creation
So Cheer up & gear up
And be a sensation.........

(Composed by Pritam Kumar Goswami)

Keep The Steering In Your Hands

You have no choice but to keep control over your life. If you fail to do that and leave things on its own, life goes out of your control. Many people allow life to go its own way and they totter like a directionless boat in the sea. The moment you decide to take steering in your hand you develop a sense of responsibility towards your action, your action start getting aligned to your dreams. There would be a situation where you will have to take risk but again you will have two choices, take risk and getting out of the problem or sitting quiet and waiting for miracles to happen.

Don't Give up to things you can't control: Have control of everything with you especially of your own and your environment. There may be many situations which are out of control like inflation, market slum but we can definitely control our thoughts and can keep the morale high.

Don't limit your capabilities: Many times we forget our real potential and gradually start limiting our own capabilities and potential through foolish excuses like "I am not educated enough, I don't know good people, I don't have ample money or my luck is not good. Even highly qualified and capable people are suffering from such 'Blocked mindset'. This mental blockage stops the flow of thoughts, we stop getting ideas and start committing unforced mistakes.

Don't give up to Fears & apprehensions: God has given us power and emotions of love but not fear. Whenever we come across the odd situations that means they are not created by god but god has definitely given us enough power to face those situations. If you have fear you should focus to "Remove fear of Failure". ***It is better to try and fail rather than not trying at all.***

You should become the person what you want to be.

Keep excuses away from your life: Don't ever let problem become the excuse. You should accept your mistakes, incompetence and incapability, but leave them behind. You can do this provided you have the right attitude.

Don't leave things on destiny: In crisis, people tend to follow astrologers, religious gurus, and so many such things. Don't ever allow such people to control your life. You are the only person who can take charge of your own life and has the ability to change the scenario. There is a saying in Bible "If you have the belief equivalent to small particle then you say a mountain not to be there. It won't be there"

Make It Happen & Become The Person You Want To Be

Amidst all uncertainties and dicey situations you need to explore the possibilities to come out of it. There is solution to all problems in life, we need to reach to the solution through free flowing thoughts. On an average a human mind perceives 20000 thoughts in a day but unfortunately most of them are negative. If we work towards possibility thinking it really works and plenty of thoughts which we perceive provides us the desired solution.

I am repeating this story once again.

A young girl with numerous dreams in her eyes aspired to be an astronaut reaching out to the galaxies and vast sky above. In her early childhood while being on the terrace she shared her indomitable dream of going to space. Coming from small town like Karnal (India) attaining that goal was exceedingly difficult. When she was 7-8 years old she used to stare in the sky. Her eyes used to search something in the sky. While looking at the sky she always said to her mother "Mom, I want to go there, Mom one day I will reach there" and her mom used to smile on her silly talks. But she was adamant, she proved that how perseverance, hard work, vision and killer instinct drove her to USA where she became a part of NASA and served there for years together. The killer instinct again turned the fortunes to her when she got selected as part of the voyage Columbia leaving for space.

Today **"Kalpana Chawla"** stands as an amazing example of how one's curiosity and dreams can take him/her to the destination.

Another Stunning Example of Possibility Thinking

Henry Ford was born in a field. When he was 16 he left the farming and worked as mechanic in Detroit. He became the foreman in Edison Company and keep on marching ahead till the time he became the Chief Engineer. Once he had a chance to see Edison and when he saw asked a question that if petrol could be a good fuel for car or not. Edison was in hurry and said "Yes" without thinking. Henry was committed. Finally after eleven years he invented a Car" Tin Lizy" He was criticized like anything but he kept on working and waited till the end of 11th year when the car was ready for the launch.

Mind is an obedient slave, whatever thoughts you give to it, it works on it. Even if we think that the idea has 1% chance of success, then remember that only our mind has the calibre to make that 1% a 100%. Every coin represents two sides: success and failure. But failures are stepping stones to success. Hence both the sides of the coin ultimately represent **success**. *That is the ultimate power of possibility thinking.*

The Dangerous Act

The Most dangerous act in the world is when somebody is lacking the energy and taking negative decision in adverse phase, which even can't be reversed.

During the tough times people generally lose their ability to see future with an optimistic attitude. They start thinking negatively about their tomorrow. They concentrate on today's problem instead of tomorrow's opportunities. By doing this they not only distort today's possibility but also lose the beauty of tomorrow.

The Power of Your Mind

**"Rarely you succeed in the first attempt,
Rarely you fail in all the attempts."**

There is hardly anybody on this earth whom we call an achiever and who got success in very first attempt. There are plenty of people who got success after many failures. It hardly matters that you are young or aged. If you want to be successful you ought to have courage to move forward. It's a game of mastering your subconscious mind to make the conscious mind move in right direction. The reiteration of the thoughts strengthens the move of sub-conscious mind to make those thoughts the reality.

Passion to Succeed

A success story may start with a dream. But to reach its Zenith, there are many other factors involved and one of them is passion.

Many years ago, Shahrukh Khan declared that one day he'll rule Mumbai. And today he's the King Khan of Bollywood. Car designer Dilip Chhabria confesses that he worked endlessly and tirelessly for about a decade making car accessories so as to raise money for his designing studio.

We all dream and we all hope that our dreams will turn into reality some day. We like them because of the Passion with which they pursued their dreams.

One needs to be 'obsessively passionate' as passion can vary, but obsession can't.

Famous actor Manoj Bajpai says,' to make the dream a reality, you need loads of patience, self-belief and the most important of all is the ability to face criticism on your face.

For these achievers, reaching their goal was merely a milestone crossed in the journey of life. As Manoj Bajpai puts it this way," My dream was never materialistic. It's an evolving journey; I grow as I live every moment of my Dream".

Passion as a Profession

Prasad fell from a vertical height of 80 ft while mountaineering at the Dudhsagar waterfalls in Goa. He broke most of the bones in his body. 12 days later, when he gained consciousness, his doctors swore he would never climb again. A year and a half later, this young man went on to do what was considered impossible. He became the first Goan to scale Mount Kedardome at 22,410 ft… that too, in a world record-breaking time of 10 hrs 20 minutes for the final stretch.

Twelve years later, Prasad Joshi is Goa's numero uno as an adventure activity trainer. The exploratory challenges of Mother Nature were always a passion for Prasad. A B.Com graduate, Prasad was an average student who excelled in sports and mimicry. The family ran a teahouse and a school canteen. While looking after the family business, Prasad made rapid strides in hiking, trekking and Mountaineering… and his passion turned into his profession.

Many mocked him… Prasad was ridiculed for relying on earning through his hobby. The voices of disapproval got shriller after his accident. Prasad says, "Nobody can conquer death. Life is a risk anyway so why not die doing something worthwhile. This view became stronger after my accident that proved to me that I had been reborn to do great things." He underwent all necessary training to excel in what was initially just a hobby. He stood first in India for rock-climbing competition held at Tekhla. He underwent the instructors' course for Rafting as well as Advanced Mountaineering Degree Course. With adventure tourism making good business sense, Prasad's infatuation with his hobby is now fully justified.

Too often, we approach careers in a one-dimensional way, looking at what is available. Surely, we can draw inspiration from Prasad. But to transform our passion into a profession, we must be able to envision the various dimensions that it contains. We can develop new facets in our passion and transform it into a profession. Eventually we can develop new passion for our chosen profession.

Passionate People : They Didn't Give Up

"Ever tried. Ever failed. No matter.
Try Again. Fail again. Fail better."
- Samuel Beckett

1. As a young man, Abraham Lincoln went to war a captain and returned a private. Afterwards, he was a failure as a businessman. As a lawyer in Springfield, he was too impractical and temperamental to be a success. He turned to politics and was defeated in his first try for the legislature, again defeated in his first attempt to be nominated for congress, defeated in his application to be commissioner of the General Land Office, defeated in the senatorial election of 1854, defeated in his efforts for the vice-presidency in 1856, and defeated in the senatorial election of 1858. At about that time, he wrote in a letter to a friend, "I am now the most miserable man living. If what I feel were equally distributed to the whole human family, there would not be one cheerful face on the earth."
2. Winston Churchill failed sixth grade. He was subsequently defeated in every election for public office until he became Prime Minister at the age of 62. He later wrote, "Never give in, never give in, never, never, never, never - in nothing, great or small, large or petty - never give in except to convictions of honor and good sense. Never, Never, Never, Never give up."
3. Socrates was called "an immoral corrupter of youth" and continued to corrupt even after the sentence of death was imposed on to him. He drank the hemlock and died corrupting.

4. Charles Darwin gave up a medical career and was told by his father, "You care for nothing but shooting, dogs and rat catching." In his autobiography, Darwin wrote, "I was considered by all my masters and my father, a very ordinary boy, rather below the common standard of intellect." Clearly, he evolved.

"Our greatest glory is not in never falling but in rising every time we fall."

- Confucius

5. Albert Einstein did not speak until he was 4-years-old and did not read until he was 7. His parents thought he was "sub-normal," and one of his teachers described him as "mentally slow, unsociable, and adrift forever in foolish dreams." He was expelled from school and was refused admittance to the Zurich Polytechnic School. He did eventually learn to speak and read.
6. When Bell telephone was struggling to get started, its owners offered all their rights to Western Union for $100,000. The offer was disdainfully rejected with the pronouncement, "What use could this company make of an electrical toy."

"Only those who dare to fail greatly can achieve greatly."

- Robert F. Kennedy

7. Babe Ruth is famous for his past home run record, but for decades he also held the record for strikeouts. He hit 714 home runs and struck out 1,330 times in his career (about which he said, "Every strike brings me closer to the next home run."). And didn't Mark McGwire break that strikeout record? (John

Wooden once explained that winners make the most errors.)

8. After Carl Lewis won the gold medal for the long jump in the 1996 Olympic games, he was asked to what he attributed his longevity, having competed for almost 20 years. He said, "Remembering that you have both wins and losses along the way. I don't take either one too seriously."

"Our achievements speak for themselves. What we have to keep track of are our failures, discouragements, and doubts. We tend to forget the past difficulties, the many false starts, and the painful groping. We see our past achievements as the end result of a clean forward thrust, and our present difficulties as signs of decline and decay."

- Eric Hoffer

9

TIME – "The Treasure of Life"

Time is the coin of your life. It is the only coin you have, and only you can determine how it will be spent. Be careful lest you let other people spend it for you.

- Carl Sandburg

The element called time is the most invaluable treasure we have. Why I call it "Treasure"? Actually our life is expressed in terms of time. Time is our life. I always believed that I am capable of doing anything and attaining whatever I dream of, but the only constraint is time. I always feel that time is too short to accomplish so many things. Time has no beginning or end. Time moves at its own pace. Time cannot be modified or customized as per personal needs. Neither does time wait for anyone nor does it differentiate between a king and a beggar. Time is an abstract resource neither earned nor borrowed. It is bestowed upon us by the almighty God.

We generally observe animals spending their lives just for the sake of spending it. They have time but no motive. They have life but no freedom to make use of that life. At times it is found that even human beings live their life in the similar manner- aimless and devoid of the zeal to live it. I have seen such people who take their lives so casually as if they have millions of years to live and enjoy. In this supersonic world everything has taken up speed. With the shrinking of distance and time, time has come out to be a dominant factor of our life. We can Make or Break our life simply by choosing how we spend our personal property-**Time**!! It is only the 'way how we use time' that can differentiate us from rest of the world. But very few people are aware of this fact.

"The common man is not concerned about the passage of time. The man of talent is driven by it."

- Shoppenhauer

Let's understand how our time is generally spent! Daily you wake up, do your routine tasks, go to your office, spend your day working there, come back home have your dinner and go to sleep. Not all the days but most of the days of our life go in the similar fashion. Most of our days come in the count of normal days. Most of the days of our life we spend doing nothing special. And that is how life passes on. With the passing of every day what ends up is an opportunity to go beyond the shackles of routine chains. With the passing of every day we lose 86400 seconds allotted to us to make our life better. With the passing of every day just as another day we wipe off the chances of getting a step ahead. And ultimately we lose the opportunity of carving our lives the finest way.

Thus every tick-tick of the clock is actually the tick-tick of our life machine. Moving time is actually the passing of life which keeps on indicating us that we are slowly moving towards our death. Managing life is all about managing time. Each one of us manages life. It's not optional. Time is the gift of God to us. It is the most precious gift that we all have and God the almighty has done justice by providing each one of the same amount of time. We all get equal 24 hours, each hour filled with 60 precious minutes and every minute containing 60 equal seconds. The law of equality reflected by God in this gift is worth admiration.

You would have heard people making such remarks and even yourself complaining in the similar manner: if I had time I would have completed my target? Had it been 1 hour more in a day I would have played golf daily? If I had time for myself I would have become a good singer? If I had time I would have completed this research? Had there been a few more days I would have performed better? There is no end to such remarks. There is no end to this quest for more time....There is no end to such demands....... It seems there is no upper limit within which target can be done. Time management is an art not of dealing with the upper limit but of dealing with the lower limits of finishing the targets. Getting more things done in a given time rather than using all the time to do a single thing is managing time in true sense.

Most Valuable Resource: Time

"Time is what we want most, but... what we use worst."

- Willaim Penn

Time is the most important resource in the world. You can earn money, fame, name, recognition, status, talents, skills, qualifications & anything & everything on this earth ......but just can you earn time??? Is it possible to purchase time by money or can you barter with Lord to give you a few more seconds to live, in exchange of your qualifications or talents!! No ..... In fact earning money, fame, name & recognition also demand time from you.

Time is the resource that is limited and if this resource is not available nothing else can be earned. Time is the most invaluable thing you hold in your hands. We all don't know how many seconds more to go in our lives but we certainly are aware about the fact that we all have a limited stock of these seconds and that no matter what; this stock once consumed cannot be refilled or recharged.

Time is money, time is more than money. Time is life!!!

Just wonder the way the needle of the clock moves second by second …our life moves breath by breath….. how we choose to live each second of our life is the way how we choose to spend our precious breaths. Time moves on and with it moves our life!! Time defines you. How you make use of this precious resource ultimately determines the altitudes you touch, the new carves you add on to your life, and the more meaningful you make your living. What is once lost can be regained- Money, power, status, and so on can be renewed but what cannot be earned back is time.

"Time = life; therefore, waste your time and waste your life, or master your time and master your life."

- Alan Lakein

Time is the invaluable resource available with each one of us!!

Uniqueness of Time

Time is an ultimate unique resource in itself.

"The Future is something which everyone reaches at the rate of sixty minutes an hour, whatever he does, whoever he is".

- C.S. Lewis

Here are few properties of time and we all are well versed with them, still I am narrating to reinforce the value of time.

It's equal to all: Same parameters of time (hours, minutes & seconds) are applicable on the entire universe indiscriminately.

It is personalized: Your time is yours. Neither can you share or transfer your time to anyone nor can anyone else do so. Every minute, every moment that you have in your stock is engraved by your name. You are the owner of your time stock.

It can't be rented or stolen: Neither can you rent time nor can it be stolen. It is true that there are many time stealers but as in case of money we see that if you keep your money loose it can be stolen by people, similarly if you let your time easily to people it gets stolen from your 'self'. Nobody can steal your time without your permission.

It is indispensable: Time is the crux, the core. Time ensures the very existence of your life. Time is the most significant resource meant to be dealt prudently.

It is limited: Time is neither scarce nor is it in abundance. But each one of us has limited seconds to go in our life after which our life would be discharged. And the reverse counting started the day we were born. So it is only the limited time period that we need to manage properly. The later we realize the lesser it gets!

It is irreversible: Time moves on and on, no turning back, no stoppages, no breaks and no reverses. It's only a one-way straight forward road. If you miss a train today you may catch it tomorrow, it might not change the situation for you as it appears. But dear friends, if you observe it carefully, it has caused a major change; one complete day is deducted from your life by then.

You may stop but time moves on: You may stop a clock, and may be you stop all the clocks of this world to ignore the movement of time, but will this solve your problem? I may stop working, time never stops for anyone, no matter in what situation you may be time has to move on!

Hours to minutes & minutes to seconds

Most time is wasted, not in hours, but in minutes. A bucket with a small hole in the bottom gets just as empty as a bucket that is deliberately emptied.

- Paul J. Meyer

Just analyze your daily routine. You consume all the 24hrs in a very systematic manner making sure that you do not waste your time at all. You wake up and go to office, work there, by evening you return back home, freshen up and have your meals; that's how you end up the day. It seems absolutely perfect that you did not waste any time at all. May be the other day there is a power cut in your office and your 2 hrs get wasted that day. But that doesn't happen frequently and nor thus such things happen daily. This means you consume all your 24 hrs with due care!! Does it also mean that you consume your 1440 minutes of the day also fully?? Mathematically this statement may appear to be correct but in our practical life this statement fails at few points. Recall the minutes spent on a call, or may be gossiping with some colleague in office, may be surfing on net and many similar situations wherein time in small slots consumed easily and unnoticeably. And to be very honest to ourselves such wastage of time occurs daily. When even a single coin falls out of our wallet we desperately search it out. This means even a single coin is important for us. Then why not we care for our minutes in the same manner? Why is it that we don't care for our each and every minute gifted to us by God? Why are we so very casual with our minutes that ultimately form hours and life? It is not long duration hours that we need to manage but small period time slots that our measured in minutes need more of our attention. To win a race every single second counts. To fill an ocean every single drop counts and hence to make our life every single moment counts.

Thus you can very easily interpret how those few minutes of daily contribution to time waste snatches away a very big part of our life. All what is required is to observe your time fillers first and then gradually reduce them & use such time to add on more value to your life.

The bad news is time flies. The good news is you're the pilot!!!

Time Stealers

Many small acts that unknowingly form part of our day-to-day routine steal out our precious moments of the day. Understanding such factors is must in order to prohibit or limit them.

There is one kind of robber whom the law does not strike at, and who steals what is most precious to men: time.

- Napoleon

Looking for Lost Things: Indiscipline, careless attitude & due to haste we fail to keep a track of things, consequently wasting time in searching them. A study revealed that an average human being spends one year of his life to find lost things.

Laziness: We all have dreams and desires. We all have thoughts to become somebody big in our life. But then most of us end up becoming just the normal human being, because to get somewhere you need to move from your present position. You need to act in the direction of your dreams. But lethargic attitude leads us nowhere. When tomorrow seems more feasible than today, we lose our time.

Interruptions: At times such happenings may occur that may obstruct our planning. Such situations may arise which do not seem to be important but become urgent and demands our time. Such unavoidable situations eat up lot of our time.

Trying to carry load by yourself: When we prefer doing all the work by our own, we avoid delegating the work to others, we end up giving more time to things than they hardly deserve.

Regretting & Daydreaming: Not being present minded, being lost in the thoughts of past snatch away the present from you.

Procrastination: Causing unnecessary delay is another time stealer which occurs often.

Personal negative attitude: negativity kills the willingness of a person to fulfil his ambition. Negative feeling consumes a lot of energy and lot of time is wasted in it.

Failing to understand the problem: Haste is waste. Without understanding the root cause of the problem we keep on putting time in it and getting frustrated. Give some time to understand the problem and you will see the problem getting resolved faster.

Failing to know the list of priorities: When we are unable to decide what to do first, when we fail to understand the priority of things, we end up messing the things. Such a state leads to confusion and reduces our efficiency, consequently doing things becomes more time consuming.

One of the best ways to stay out of confusion is as follows:

Clear your desk: The clarity of desks avoids mugging up of thoughts in your mind

Phone Calls: Making note of the core point of the conversation, making it brief & precise, to the point. Avoid making too many calls.

Managing the Seconds

"Take care of the minutes and the hours will take care of themselves."

- Lord Chesterfield

Every second has to be utilized by us. But it is not possible for all of us to utilize it effectively. Or in other words time needs to be managed.

There are four steps:

STEP 1: Analyze where your time goes;

If you miss even ten rupee note, your mind will not be stable till you find out the missed note. You may feel that you have lost some worthy thing. Some will become even nervous. But most of us never bothered about the time we have wasted or time that we have lost in doing unproductive works or sitting idle.

To manage time effectively, first of all you have to look yourself how your time is being spent. You have to write down how you have spent time for a day, week, and month. If you go through the list you can identify how far you have spent time usefully, effectively, most of the time you might have used time in an ineffective way. While you are doing this analysis, you can classify the works you have done according to the following category;

1. Works that are being done on routine basis.
2. Others could have done Works that have been done by me.
3. Works that are urgently to be done to meet my objectives.
4. Works that can be done at a later time also.
5. Works that are to be done now itself, which can't be postponed.
6. Time spent being idle.
7. Time spent for unproductive works.

STEP 2: Decide where your time should go:

After analyzing your time how it normally goes or being spent, you can identify how much time is available to you to do activities other than your routine activities. If you are doing only routine activities you cannot grow or develop as a better individual, to say you will be an ordinary person. To become Extra-ordinary person you have to set objectives and you have to work for meeting those objectives.

After time analysis you can allocate time for activities that will enable you to meet your goals. You have to allocate time. You have to prioritize our timing in the following way;

First you have to do activities that are Important & urgent.

Then you have to do activities that are Important but not urgent.

Then you have to do activities that are not Important but urgent.

Finally you can do activities that are not important and not urgent but needed to be done.

STEP 3: Identify Time wasters:

While you are doing activities you may encounter difficulties / hurdles that will not allow you to spare time for doing activities and it will delay your works such things are called time wasters. There are numerous time wasters. It is very difficult to do activities without time waster's effect. One has to identify it as it comes on their way of execution. Many of us are not aware of our habits and time spent in small daily routine. I still see few friends spending couple of hours in the morning in getting ready for office and few of them take half an hour in shaving only. Many of them are addicted to chatting on internet. One such friend having a jam packed schedule is busy on chat till 2 in the night and has no time for his health and family.

STEP 4: Master your time wasters:

It is difficult to eliminate time wasters, but it can be mastered by proper planning.

Once I went to invite the superintendent of police to invite for a function being organized by local chapter of JCI. The moment I entered in his chamber along with my friends, he rose from the chair, received the Invitation and disposed us quickly. After coming out of his room I was confused if he stood up in our respect or what. I could not understand for what he did. I came to know at a later date that it is an effective method of disposing of long winding persons. Had he not rose from his chair, he had to offer seats for all of us and spend some time with us. There was every possibility that we might have put up a demand, which would have required some more time to dispose. All things were avoided by rising from his chair. This is a perfect example how to master time wasters.

Say no to Procrastination

Procrastination is a disease. It's nothing but postponing today's task on tomorrow and when tomorrow comes that task becomes an urgent one. You may be addicted with urgency syndrome. You never look at the importance of the task because we have no priority system. You enjoy working under urgency pressure. Here are few examples:

- Most students get serious towards studies only a month before exam.
- Many of us go and pay the electricity and telephone bills only when deadline approaches.
- Many people refill fuel tank of their cars when needle reaches to empty signal.
- Most people file their income tax returns when due date is very few days away.

The result is evident. People spend most of their life struggling with those urgent tasks. They hardly have any time to think and work on their goals and priorities. They keep on moving because something is pushing them, they are moving not by choice but by default. That's the reason why we see very few people in the world who dominate the factor called time, who carry their schedule by their choice.

I have learnt a lot from my father to work on priorities, I have never seen him battling with urgencies. He is a retired banker and I don't remember a single instance when he reached his office late even by 5-10 minutes. Whenever he travels his bag is ready one day earlier. Whenever he receives a bill, it's paid in next two days. He is so systematic and proactive, that's why he could grow that much in life.

The result of procrastination is worst. We keep on postponing important things of our life on tomorrow. Slowly and gradually we start scrapping our important things from pending list. The common man is busy whole life doing something or other but achievement is none. Choice is yours. You must develop a habit of keeping a list of your priorities and if you can finish non urgent tasks today, finish them. You will have lot of free time to think for your growth and expansion after leaving procrastination. Eventually, you will have a lot of peace in your life.

Techniques to Manage Time:

The following techniques help save the seconds that are so critical for our focused approach towards our life.

ROUTINE – "Set it"

One of the main problems that we face at time is that we tend to spend each day with a casual approach. In such a situation even our routine activities are mishandled by us. No proper sequencing consumes more of our time. Hence it is must to set the routine first. This would not only gives a smooth way to do our day-to-day activities but will also helps us identify our free time slots in a day.

'Plan – Your Work'

"Living your life without a plan is like watching television with someone else holding the remote control."

- Peter Turla

Drawing a rough sketch of what has to be done puts us in a better position to beware of what next has to be done. Planning helps us in mental preparedness and once that is done its only the implementation part that remains thereafter.

'Delegate- your Task'

It's unquestionable that things need to be delegated to others to finish of the work on time and be in a position to do many things at a time. Delegation not only helps in division of work but it helps your mind be free of minute details of the work to be done, which could be ordinarily done by anyone besides you.

Procrastination- 'Say no to it'

The biggest enemy that stands tall on our way to success is procrastination. It is the killer of time. Once you start delaying there is no limit to it.

PLAN:

Priorities – set it

Law of Parkinson & pruto – implement it

Allocate time- Use day planner

No time- Never say, plan your time

Priorities: each one of us has 'N' number of tasks to do, a number of dreams to be fulfilled and many goals to achieve. But it is not possible to move in all directions simultaneously.

We need to do things one by one, step by step. Thus it is must to prioritize the things as per their importance and urgency. Such sequencing helps you ensuring timely completion of all the work and aids in goal accomplishment.

"If you want to make good use of your time,
you've got to know what's most important
and then give it all you've got."
- Lee Iacocca

Law of Parkinson & Pruto: The 80-20 rule of Parkinson & Pruto states that 80% reward comes from 20% of effort. Hence these 20% efforts need more of our time than the remaining stuff. The focus on this 20% part ensures a better success ratio and hence differentiating between the various things is must. We need to understand that not all tasks deserve the same devotion in terms of time. Some tasks need our expertise and some tasks are simply normal ones. Giving more time to the significant ones will ensure a better success rate.

Allocate time & Use day planner: when a train starts for a journey from the source to the destination, it passes by various stations. Proper scheduling of the journey is done by allocating time to various stations and mentioning the stoppage timings at various rest points. Similarly in our day-to-day journey of life allocation of time among various works helps giving a rough sketch in our mind how the work can be finished and how much time would it call for. A day- to –day planning helps us control our time at minute levels too. In such a situation we are in the position to keep a check on our minutes and seconds as well. We automatically become more vigilant about our moves throughout the day and try hard to stick to the plan and ensure its accomplishment by the day end.

Never say, plan your time: Don't give your time to words better perform on the platform and prove your saying. Senseless wastage of time in speaking not only eats up time but also consumes your energy which may be better utilized in working. Hence prefer 'doing' rather than 'saying'.

SAVING: (Take time out from time wasters)

'Saving' is a simple way of prudent investment of time. Saving doesn't imply that stop the clock from moving ahead, try to hold back time. It means better utilization of time. A person can save time from time wasters. The following steps ensure proper saving of time:

Set up fixed routine: A pre-scheduled routine helps getting things done faster. It becomes easier to plan what could be done and when. Routine task generally are not too time-consuming. But no planning of them leads to a haphazard situation ultimately taking longer time than what should have been consumed. Hence the foremost important aspect is to fix up the daily routine to ensure optimum utilization of time.

Act before important becomes urgent: Things done on time and things done before time have different impacts. Procrastinating tasks till the deadline reaches converts the important tasks to urgent. And it is in such situations that we understand the true significance of time management. It is better to manage before than to regret later.

Visualize and plan your work: Forecasting the things, envisaging all the possible situations help us prepare in advance accordingly. Planning for the future saves a lot of our time and help us approach all the things systematically thus putting things in a sequenced manner.

Interruption can be avoided if analyzed: many a times it is possible to predict the upcoming problems and hence one should prepare accordingly. When we know a problem may arise, the solution should be immediately worked out rather than waiting for the problem to first occur, then cry over the spilt milk and thereafter search for the solution. Being proactive is the key to ensure problem-proof working. Problems can only stretch the time or slow down the working. So it's better to get them resolved before time.

Never sail in two boats: When we try to work simultaneously in two different directions, we reach nowhere. None of the tasks gets completed and ultimately the time goes all wasted. In such a state of confusion when we are unable to decide which work to do first, it is better to evaluate both the tasks in terms of their importance and thereby choosing one task out of the options, getting it finished and thereafter switching to the other one. Such a systematic approach ensures completion of all the important tasks sequentially without any compromise.

Get the things done: No doubts when you work you ensure the BEST. But it is not feasible every time to do every single activity by your own. At times it is the need of the hour to delegate things to others. Distribution of work helps reduce the work burden and the work gets completed on time. Remember, its an art to get the work done by the people and ensuring proper quality control as well.

Balance Sheet of Life

Let's see if an average human being lives for 70 years, where the time is spent in years in the whole life, it's interesting and mind blowing too:

Sleeping – 22 Yrs　　Childhood – 3 Yrs.
Education – 6 Yrs　　Routine work – 7 Yrs.

Gossiping/ Entertainment -4 Yrs	Job/Business - 10Yrs
Travelling – 3 Yrs.	Daily commuting – 2 Yrs
Medication – 3 Yrs	Social Resp. – 2 Yrs
Time wasters – 3 Yrs	Old age – 4 Yrs
Searching Lost Things-1 Year	

The above stated balance sheet can be modified as per your will. For example a very good friend of mine has a habit to make use of his travelling time by making all the calls during travelling. I still remember when I was doing Post Graduate Diploma in Business Administration few years back and due to my hectic schedule and lots of travelling had no time to study. I planned properly and I finished 75% of my PGDBA studies during my travelling itself and I scored more than 70% in exams. Similarly there is no standard time period for sleep. It is how we train our body the very same way it would behave. Most people sleep for 8 hours a day and waste one third of their life in sleeping only. I have seen many people around me who sleep for 5-6 hours a day, work efficiently and stay physically fit, at contrast I have also seen such people who in spite of sleeping for 8 or more hours a day are ineffective at their work and carry many diseases in their body. It's a simple common sense when we have limited capital and various investment options we invest in the alternative which seems more attractive to us. In the same manner we have multiple options in front of us to invest our time willingly for the well thought purpose. It's up to us which alternative we prefer. We can't increase the span of our life but surely we can reshuffle the balance sheet of our life. We can get some time out from wasteful activities and invest the saved time in prioritized activities. Hence this balance sheet can be customized and used as an effective tool to design the roadmap of our life and hence selectively make use of the invaluable resource 'TIME'.

Time can't be accumulated. It has no past and future time can't be used in advance like credit cards. Time is in present. We should live in present and present should be well directed and well planned.

Translation of a Sanskrit Poem

"The joy of growth,
The splendour of action,
The glory of power.
For yesterday is but a memory
And tomorrow is only a vision;
But today well lived
Makes every yesterday a memory of happiness
And every tomorrow a vision of hope
Look well, therefore to this day"

10

The Bond of Love

"One is remembered for what one does for others; not for what, one does for self."

- M. K. Soni

Human life calls for a reason. No one on this earth is present without a reason. Think about this- do we live our lives only for our own self? The answer is a big NO. Every person has a reason to live, that goes beyond his own self. We work to feed our families. We put efforts to make things easier for our family, friends and society. Kids study hard to become successful in their lives and make their parents feel proud of them. A company consistently looks forward to go miles ahead in serving its customers. Observe every single life around you and you'll find a reason that it lives to add on better moments in other lives. Thus the interpersonal aspect of life is the core of human heart.

Relations have always been precious pearls to ornament our lives and make it more valuable. In past when people lived a simple life they had ample time for others. People were so concerned and caring, for their near & dear ones. Their relations were filled with warmth & hospitality. They always worked for a genuine cause to strengthen their relations with everyone. With the passage of times things have changed. The amount and quality of progress we have made in the past 30 years is quite amazing. Life is made much easier and smoother. Better & faster ways of communication have shrunk time & distance. Technology has simplified our lives. Every single advancement in life, has indeed provided people with more time for themselves than before.

But just look at the irony: we try to be in touch with friends staying thousands of miles away from us but we are not bothered about our family member sitting next to us. Indeed we have reached the space and moon but don't take initiative to ring the doorbell of our neighbour. We try to understand the strangers who come in our life but we fail to understand our own life partner. Are we really loosing the bond of love or genuine feelings for a relationship?

In the blaze of multitude of relations the pivotal relations of our life have become dormant. Tight working schedules, hectic routine, more ambitious targets, ever-increasing competition, technological advancements and more of mechanization have derelict our heart from the core necessity of human life- relation. It's not that people don't have relations now, it's just that good, sound and strengthened relations are rare to find today. Every relation demands time & space. And in such a fast moving life the thread of relation gets stretched & weathered out.

"Once I was conducting a seminar for senior executives of a company and while taking a session on relationships I asked one participant, Ya, tell me on how many persons you have been dependent since morning i.e. who helped you in various tasks of yours? He thought for a while, stood still for some time and when he started speaking, he quite much surprised himself, for we don't pretty much realize the people

we should be thankful to until and unless we give thought to it. From morning to noon he had many people who directly or indirectly contributed to his day e.g. his wife, his son, the milkman, the news paper hawker, the servant, the driver, the office servant, his colleagues and so on. He said, "Well, I am dependent upon my wife, who woke me up in the morning, my daughter who prepared my morning tea, my mother who got me the news paper, the laundry guy who washed & ironed my clothes, again my wife who is the sole person who will get the credit for me being punctual with everything kept arranged, my driver who dropped me in time, the gatekeeper who opened the gate for me, the liftman who further helped me and of course my company officials who have organized this seminar to add value to my life, and How can I forget my colleagues who are giving me best of the companionship."

My dear friends each one of us is dependent on dozens of people everyday but we hardly realize this fact. We are living in the era of technology where human emotions are getting eroded every day, life becoming self centred, dependency on machines is growing up and up but as a human being my dependency on human beings, my emotions, my feelings, my happiness and sorrows, our need to share our feelings are still basic necessity. Tell me one thing if I ask you to be inside the room alone with best of the luxuries and with favourite time pass of yours like best of the videos, books or wines, how many days you can happily stay inside the room, hardly a day. We desperately need people around to help and to be helped.

Just wonder how a child enjoys with his friends at school. He plays with them, he laughs out loud, he talks to them, and he is actually full of life then. But the day his friend's are absent he feels so lonely, he feels so low and left out. Same is the situation of the entire human life. When we have people around us we feel accepted & loved.

We can share our feelings & ease out our heart to them. But the moment we are alone, everything seems so gloomy, so dull, and so lifeless. It is the consequence of this stage in life that people lose direction, stop loving themselves & are clouded by stress & depression.

Essence of a Relationship

People like us not because of the way we look or we dress or we speak or how affluent or famous we are. People like us for our behaviour, for what and how we make them feel. We may be literate enough but if we can't read and understand people it's all a waste. Different people are to be treated differently; they have their different needs, mindsets and emotional patterns. Understanding people and their emotions don't need any expertise or some qualification in human relations. What it needs is a thoughtfulness for others and empathy. I hope none of us missed on a milestone bollywood movie of "Munna Bhai MBBS", it's a personal favourite of mine and the hero in spite of being illiterate and anti social element uses the art of winning people's heart.

Eleven Amazing Facts You Probably Never Knew or Thought About

1. At least 5 people in this world love you so much they would die for you.
2. At least 15 people in this world love you in some way.
3. The only reason anyone would ever hate you is because they want to be just like you.
4. A smile from you can bring happiness to anyone, even if they don't like you.
5. Every night, someone thinks about you before they go to sleep.

6. You mean the world to someone.
7. If not for you, someone may not be living.
8. Someone that you don't even know exists loves you.
9. Always remember the compliments you received. Forget about the rude remarks.
10. Always tell someone how you feel about them; you will feel much better when they know.
11. If you have a great friend, take the time to let them know that they are great.

If you work on the chemistry of relations keeping the above 11 gems in your mind your life will be smoothen by the soothing and pleasing relations you would be carrying with you.

True Affection

"I would like to share something on the 'nature of love'. I once had a friend who was very close to me. Once when he was sitting at the edge of a swimming pool, he filled the palm of his hand with a little water and held it before me, and said this: "You see this water carefully contained on my hand? It symbolizes Love." As long as you keep your hand caringly open and allow it to remain there, it will always be there. However, if you attempt to close your fingers around it and try to posses it, it will spill through the first cracks it finds. This is the greatest mistake that people do when they meet love...they try to posses it, they demand, they expect... and just like the water spilling out of your hand, Love will retrieve from you.

For love is meant to be free, you can't change its nature. If there are people you love, allow them to be free beings."

It might sound simple, but it is a lesson that may take a lifetime to truly practice. It is the secret to true love.

To truly practice it, you must sincerely feel no expectations from those who you love, and yet an unconditional caring.

Trust Builds the Bond

TRUST is a very important factor for all relationships. When trust is broken, it is the end of the relationship. Lack of trust leads to suspicion, suspicion generates anger, anger causes enmity and enmity may result in separation.

A telephone operator told me that one day she received a phone call. She answered, "Public Utilities Board." There was silence. She repeated, "PUB." There was still no answer. When she was going to cut off the line, she heard a lady's voice, "Oh, so this is PUB. Sorry, I got the number from my Husband's pocket but I do not know whose number it is." Without mutual trust, just imagine what will happen to the couple if the telephone operator answered with just "hello" instead of "PUB".

Giving importance to other's feelings and making them feel important is the key to a long-lasting sound relationship. One feels more valued and accepted if you give them a patient hearing and try to understand their side of the situation. Listening leads to a better understanding and once you understand a person fully; you can direct your relation as you want. You actually develop acceptability among others. You are then in a position to inspire & influence people. And this adds on more depth to your relations.

Echoing Relations

Everything that you give in this world echoes back to you. By giving tears none of us ever earned a smile. By inflicting hatred all around none of us could ever had a feel of love. It's a very simple natural fact: What you give, you get it back. You give smile you'll earn a smile, you give love you'll receive it too; you give faith you'll get faith around. Thus even relations are not a one-way traffic. Whatever you give you get it back. So just give what you expect from others. Treat others the way you want yourself to be treated. It's a human tendency to expect. But even a plant gives fruits only when you take proper care of it, give it apt nourishment and cultivate it throughout the season. You need to give what you actually aspire from the relation. Giving is the key to a healthy relation which most of us fail to understand.

At times, while Gardening we sometimes come across such plants that despite of getting everything required to grow, fail to respond back. It fails to grow up like other plants of the garden. When you realize that this plant is no more alive do you still water it daily like other plants? Do you still look forward for its nourishment? No!! Dear friends, no relation has ever been complete by one sided efforts. In order to give shape to a complete relation it requires an equal concern from both the sides. If you care, the other person should respond to it. If you give love the other person should actually value it, if you give, you should even take. Every relation is a 'give take' game. It is a mutual consideration that nurtures the relation to be a strong one. Whatever we give to others ultimately comes back to us.

Thinking Beyond 'Self'

A holy man was having a conversation with the Lord one day and said," Lord, I would like to know what Heaven and Hell are like.

The Lord led the holy man to two doors. He opened one of the doors and the holy man looked in. In the middle of the room was a large round table. In the middle of the table was a large pot of stew which smelled delicious and made the holy man's mouth water. The people sitting around the table were thin and sickly. They appeared to be famished. They were holding spoons with very long handles and each found it possible to reach into the pot of stew and take a spoonful, but because the handle was longer than their arms, they could not get the spoons back into their mouths. The holy man shuddered at the sight of their misery and suffering. The Lord said, "You have seen Hell."

They went to the next room and opened the door. It was exactly the same as the first one. There was the large round table with the large pot of stew which made the holy man's mouth water again. The people were equipped with the same long-handled spoons, but here the people were well nourished and plump, laughing and talking. The holy man said, "I don't understand"." It is simple said the Lord, "it requires nothing but one skill. You see, they actually learnt feed each other. While the greedy& self centered person thinks only of himself.

Do You Have A Cosmetic Personality?

No two persons on this earth are alike. Each one of us is a unique creation of God. You hold your own self-identity. At times when you look forward to establish a good bonding with someone you behave in a way different from your 'self'. You pretend not to be your 'natural' self. You actually try to hide your original identity/nature/behaviour. You pretend to be a different person just to impress the other person, or to get a better acceptance by that person. But dear friends, is that acceptance for you or is it for the 'artificial person' that you just created?

Let's take an example of cosmetics. They may help you enhance your looks and add on more grace to your appearance, but does it stay forever? Cosmetics are artificial accessories that may give you a different look temporarily but a single water spread is sufficient to get you back to your original self. Ultimately your fake looks do not stay on you forever. What stays with you forever is your original self, your natural beauty as gifted by God. Similarly just wonder how a couple tries to impress each other in the initial days of their relation. They treat each other as prince & princess. Surprisingly they behave in such a marvellous manner as if they were born flawless. But what happens gradually? As the relation grows you get to know each other better. The veil of your artificial personality sheds off gradually. And your bare original picture appears in front of your partner.

I always give an example in my seminars, A couple starts meeting each other to build a relation of marriage or love, they always try to impress each other with the cosmetic personality, they present what they don't possess and they hide which they shouldn't have. Later on when they start noticing each other's shortcomings they shatter and bonding remains no longer in the relationship. One guy goes for an interview, he tries to convey all good parts of his knowledge and personality (which in fact may not be present) and deliberately does not disclose his weaker side. The truth comes out and he loses the credibility.

If somebody can't love us at our worst, he or she doesn't have right to love us at our best. We all have some or the other weaknesses we should be transparent and open about while building relationship.

An effective relation does not need much out of me, But it needs just the natural 'ME'!!

So never ever try to fake out your personality, because it's going to lead you nowhere in the long run. 'Normal & natural' conduct is the best prescription for a healthy relation. Be your original self.

People Centric Approach

Let's answer the following few questions from ourselves:

Why do I form a relation: to give happiness or to get happiness?

What is the effect of my words on the other person?

How is a relation affected by my actions?

What are my expectations from this relation?

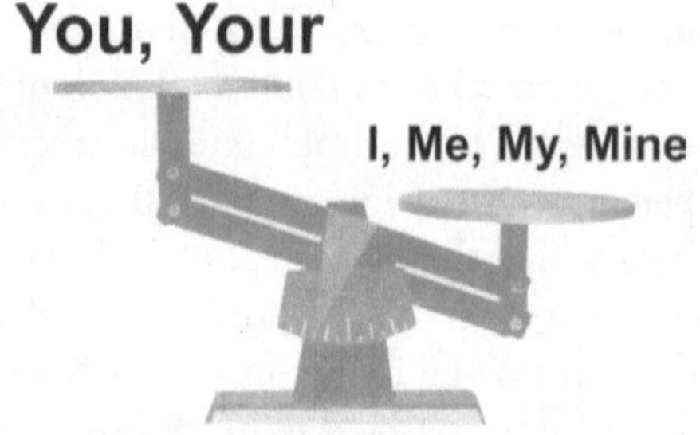

The above stated questions and many such questions can be put forth to understand why people lose relations. These questions help us analyze what we focus upon. We prefer being in the company of the people who make us feel happy. At the end of the day my words and actions should earn satisfaction to me. Thus in every sense the focus of this relation is 'Me' & 'Myself'. I live in this world to fulfil my own interest. The focus of all the relations I carry is self-centred. Let's consider an example of a company selling goods in the market. The company aspires to grow quickly in the market. It focuses on its product, keeps cost in control and starts earning huge profits.

Gradually the demand of the customer changes, customers now demand for the better version of this product. The better version requires huge investment by the company which means no profit for next two years. Thus here we face a dilemma where the aspiration of the company comes in conflict with the expectations of the customer. And if the company moves in a self-centred manner, it does not change its product, does not fulfil the expectations of the customer, soon it would lose all its customers. A hence the relation would be lost.

That is the reason why all the companies today treat Customers as King. Whatever the customer demands, he gets. By giving more importance to the customer a company tries to earn a long run relation with the customer. If a company takes care of all the needs of the customer, fulfils all his expectation from the company, the company earns a strong bonding with the customers.

Thus we see that the key to a strengthening relation is not 'Me or My self' but its 'You & Yours'. Giving the other persons that special feel, making them feel more valued & cared for- is the main ingredient of a successful relation. When the words 'me myself' get converted into 'you yourself' there is a sea change in the way we start perceiving things. We actually sprinkle in that understanding in the relation which ensures its eternality. It's all about giving more priority to others. It's all about viewing things from the other side of the fence. It's all about valuing the relation more than your own individual self.

Innermost Desire

It's an amazing beauty of human life that almost every one of us lives under the same sky, breath in the same air, walk on the same green grass, survives on the same nutrients. We are so identical in this sense. Yet we consider ourselves to be so unique from others. Each one of us lives our life as if our life is so different from others. It's so unique in itself - as if I am a very special person, as if I am totally different from this world. We treat ourselves with so much love & care and expect the same from others. We are so conscious about how the world treats us. We prefer to be in the company of the people who care for us, who love us more than others, who actually make us feel so special. It's the desire for that special treatment that brings us close to some people more than others. Thus it's a natural human instinct to be inclined towards more love, care, respect & affection.

Now just wonder that the same desire forms the core need of every heart on this earth. Thus the people we come in touch with in our lives, the people who surround us at the workplace, our family & friends all desire to get a special feel. Everyone deeply yearns for more love & care. Everyone looks forward for genuine concern & respect. There is an invisible tag around every person's neck which says 'make me feel good'. Hence the more you give the special feel to people the stronger your bondage would be. Give the shade of 'specialty' to the strings of your relations & then see the wonder happening.

Developing a beautiful relation not only requires the art of striking the chord right but it also requires you to strike the right chord.

Mind Your Words

The virus in the relation mainly comes from talking behind backs, loose talks and speaking in rude manner. It really hurts people and ruins relations as well.

We don't realize the impact of this hurting and when we hurt somebody through our words we simply escape by saying, "I didn't intend to hurt you" or "I said it in a light way", we never accept that they were actually our wrong words which caused the damage. Here is an interesting story of a Lion:

"A dense forest was surrounded by few villages, the forest was ruled by a lion, No villager was allowed to enter the forest. Whoever went to forest never returned back.

A poor man comes from other place starts living in a nearby village with his family. Once he goes to forest to cut some woods in ignorance that he will be killed by the lion. Lion came to know about that man's presence in the forest, he caught the man and told "Man you have broken the rule, hence be ready to sacrifice your life", the poor man could sense all and started apologizing. He cried, bent down on his knees and requested lion to forgive him with the words that I am new to the area and I will never commit this again. The lion somehow got convinced and he spared that man with a privilege "Look I liked your honesty and I am forgiving you for your fault but you being an honest and genuine man can come to forest and collect dry woods whenever you need. The man returned home and starts going to forest often whenever he needed woods, now he has woods more than his needs, he started selling spare woods. Over the period of few months he emerged as renowned wood seller in that area. Many people used to ask him, "Don't you feel afraid of lion?" and many such questions. One day that man arrogantly replied, hmmm….. I am not scared of lion, in fact that lion is mere a cat, he runs away the moment I enter the forest.

We live in a society where many people play the role of a postman. They are experts in communicating overheard talks to others after adding a few spices to it. One such postman communicated these words of man to the Lion. Lion got furious and repented his decision to spare that man, but he thought of teaching lesson to the man. Few days later when the man went to forest, lion caught him and furiously scolds him for his loose talks about the lion. Lion said, "My dear now no one can save your life." The man could realize his mistake and immediately apologized and touched the feet of lion. Lion thought, there is no sense in killing him, rather I should help him learning a lesson.

He told man "Look if you want to escape then hit your axe on my back". Man couldn't understand this and kept quiet for a minute. The lion once again shouted "are you hitting on my back or should I kill you?" The man in fear hit on the back of the lion with his axe, it started bleeding heavily, Lion was in pain and told to man, "Now you go back and do come after two months to meet me."

The man had terrible two months in tension that what would happen to him after two months. Exactly on completion of second month he proceeded to forest, he finds the lion and said, "As per your order I am back". Lion asked him to have a look on his injury. Man said "It's healed now, I can't see it." The lion finally tells the man "look my physical injury is healed in just two months but the injury you gave to me through your words is still in my heart and whenever I remember them it pinches me badly."

We might not have slapped somebody but knowingly or unknowingly we slap many people through our words. People may forget that real slap but it's very difficult for them to forget those bad words which we speak to hurt them.

You must watch your words and expressions, am I really hurting somebody through my words, behaviour and expression. If unknowingly you do it, immediately say sorry when you realize it.

Words are an accessory gift provided only to human beings as an added on feature to human life. Let's see how this added on feature adds essence to our life:

Words are the easiest way to express our thoughts.

Words earn us psychological satisfaction.

Words once spoken cannot be taken back.

Words expose your level of thinking and understanding too.

Words have an impact on the environment around you.

Right Speech

There is a Chinese saying which carries the meaning that "A speech will either prosper or ruin a nation." Many relationships break off because of wrong speech. When a couple is too close to each other, they always forget mutual respect and courtesy. We may say anything without considering the fact that it may hurt the other individual.

A friend and her millionaire husband visited their construction site. A worker who wore a helmet saw her and shouted, "Hi, Shelly! Remember me? We used to date in the secondary school." On the way back home, her millionaire husband teased her, "Luckily you married me. Otherwise you would have been the wife of a construction worker." She answered, "You should appreciate that you married me. Otherwise, he would have been the millionaire and not you."

Frequently exchanging such remarks plant the unfortunate seed to the relationship which will be ruined certainly. It's like Broken Egg - cannot be reversed.

The Triple Filter Test

I read a very interesting methodology in a book to abstain ourselves from useless talks about others and avoiding problems in our relations.

"One man approached a saint, "Sir I want to tell you something, it's very urgent," saint replies, "Yes tell me", The man said sir that friend of yours..", saint stopped him, "Look I have a principle in my life, I generally don't talk and listen about a person who is not present with me." The man was taken aback, He said, "Won't you listen to me even if it's important." Saint said "Of course I will, but when you pass my triple filter test, I will ask three questions and if I find all answers to be positive I will surely listen to what is in your mind?"

Saint starts interrogating the man, "My first question is "Have you ensured that the matter you are going to tell me about your friend is a fact?", Man replied, "I am not sure." Saint said "Your answer is negative, still I am giving you one more opportunity, My second question is, the matter you are going to tell me about my friend, is it related to his good or bad", The man hesitantly replies, "Sir it is something I think bit bad." Saint was bit excited and tells "Oh your second answers too goes negative, still I am giving you the final opportunity, Am I going to be benefited if I hear what you say?" Man replied "Not at all sir!!!"

Saint with the smile concludes the talk "My dear, why should I spend time in listening to a talk which is not fact, which is not related to goodness of my friend and in the end which is not going to benefit me even."

We indulge ourselves in many such talks on daily basis, we talk about who are not present with us, we talk useless things which are not true and we don't fetch any benefit out of those discussions. We spend lot of time in such talks and gossips. Finally some postman communicates the discussion to the person concerned and the relationship looses the bond.

Are You Making Enemies?

Criticism has a powerful killer instinct. No matter whatever the intention may be but the way words flow out while criticizing it works like scissors. It's easy to cut off the relation in a fraction of second through criticism. Criticism works just the way opposite to appreciation. It creates distance. It hampers mutual understanding. It reduces a person's confidence level. And above all before igniting someone else's heart you put your own heart on fire. By criticizing people you are making everlasting enemies who even after our death will curse us. In most situations we criticize people just to make fun of them or give ourselves a feeling of superiority. It doesn't help anybody.

Friendly Criticism

It does not mean we should not point out a person's mistake, we should not tell others where they went wrong. In order to make a person notice about his flaw, we need not to be blunt or sarcastic. There is a better way out to get the mistakes rectified. Criticizing people without hurting them is called positive criticism. Positive criticism is an art. One needs to ensure the following points in order to deliver the right degree of criticism:

- Good intention: Ultimate motive should be not to humiliate a person but to rectify the action.
- Isolation: Appreciation needs crowd but criticism requires isolation.

- Benefit: Never highlight the mistake but highlight the benefits he may get by correcting his mistake. Ultimately all actions will be aimed towards improvement.
- Warmth: Be a friend, be a well-wisher and then only give your suggestion, your concern would be received whole-heartedly.
- Right timing: Time & space matter a lot. Right timing & right place will communicate the exact intention behind your words.
- PCP: Praise –criticize-praise. It's a golden rule to criticism. Sandwich criticism between the words of praise helps communicate the flaws without a blunt attack on the other person.
- Make the criticism impersonal: Criticize the act not the person.
- Supply the answer: The emphasis should not be on the mistake but on the means & ways to correct the mistake & avoid its recurrence.
- No repetition: Repetition of a person's mistake again & again in your communication is nagging. It can never serve your purpose. A single note of criticism is sufficient to direct the person.

Handling Your Own Criticism

What about a situation when you find somebody criticizing you. I am impressed with a line of Dale Carnegie "Nobody kicks a dead dog." Whenever you notice somebody criticizing you, first introspect "Whether you did something wrong to somebody?" If yes, then take that criticism sportingly and correct yourself, if required apologize to the person concerned. If you think you were nowhere wrong and people are talking bad because they are envious of your growth, feel happy that you are becoming popular. No one has time to talk about an ordinary person. People, especially your competitors and colleagues, generally can't digest your progress. They will talk loose about you, just to console themselves.

Power of Appreciation

Appreciation is getting power by giving strength. It's the key to nurture a relation in the right direction. A child at home is appreciated when he does a good thing, a student in school is appreciated for his academic performance, and a company appreciates its employees through various means like promotions, more perquisites & bonus. Thus we can find this activity practically present in varied fields of our life. But the question arising here is how much is this quality reflected in my personal life? Do I also bear the art of appreciation in me?

Let's go the other way round. What happens when somebody appreciates you? How do you feel the whole day? Doesn't it give a magical joy? Isn't it that your spirits are high that day? You feel more free & happy. Not only this, you meet people cheerfully and spread more happiness around. Just one single statement of appreciation makes you feel yourself at the top of the world.

Remember everybody on the Earth is craving for appreciation and recognition. By praising others you can influence them to a great extent. The most important rule in this revolution is that whatever appreciation you do, you do it sincerely. Appreciate only when the person deserves it. An appreciation that is not genuine is considered to be flattery. Appreciation for the sake of appreciating is wrong. A true appreciation emerges right from the heart. Some tips to learn the art of appreciation are as follows:

- Be specific: Let the person know without a doubt, what he is being praised for.
- Try not to use the usual words: Wonderful, beautiful, and dynamic! Replace them with unusual words: Exceptional, remarkable, and splendid!
- Right thing at the right time to the right person results the right impact. Hence do the appreciation when required. Appreciation delayed is no appreciation at all.
- Do it as unusually as you can. Whether give a gift, send a note or even say it, make the appreciation unique. It will be remembered for a long time.
- Never combine appreciation with criticism. "I must appreciate your punctuality, but..." You are killing the importance of your words.
- Remember everyone wants to be appreciated and recognised but only genuine and true appreciation is needed.

Let's develop the mastery in appreciating people. The day you are master of appreciating people, you will start living in many hearts. People will be ready to do anything for you, it breeds loyalty. Most of us are very miser while extending appreciation, we do it when we need some favour from somebody while doing it we look at the status of the recipient. Everybody around us who is doing something for us or helping us deserves that appreciation. It doesn't cost anything and perhaps it's a big morale booster for other. The words of appreciation may be simply few words for us but a great treasure for the recipient. Let me share a true instance related to my friend:

My friend was living in a town near Bangalore. After passing higher secondary exams he was to shift to Bangalore for higher education. It was Sunday and he was supposed to leave for Bangalore that night. He went to a hair cutting saloon for hair cut where he had been going since his childhood. While sitting in saloon he was thinking that almost for the last time I will be getting haircut here. He was very much impressed with the soft behaviour, smile and dedication of the saloon owner. After coming back home, he wrote a letter of appreciation to saloon owner, drops it to post box and departs for Bangalore in the night. Couple of years later he is in hometown and with the need of hair cut he goes to same saloon. The moment he enters the saloon the owner exclaimed with joy "Sir, you… Please sit I will cut your hair first. My friend could not understand the reason and sat on the chair to get hair cut. He out of curiosity asked the owner, "Sir why are you giving me such importance and priority?" The owner replied, "In my 25 years of business, you are the only person who appreciated me and my dedication. I serve people with best of my abilities, but no one compliments and if there is some shortcoming in hair cut, people curse me. You made me feel worthy in my profession and look there the letter you sent me is framed and hanged on the wall, it's a big and life time treasure for me."

Now you can understand how magical are the words of appreciation? And to what extent they can influence people?

Power of Expression

Our expressions and words differentiate us from animals. We can smile, we can compliment, we can console and we can applaud. Some time we avoid expressing our emotions to our near and dear ones with a thought that it's implied and already known to that person. In fact each expression of your emotion, each expression of love and appreciation strengthens the bond of relation. Your mother and/or wife takes ultimate care of yours, when they cook a dish for you, how many times you go and compliment from the core of your heart? I know each one of us have immense amount of love for our parents, brother, sister, kids, spouse and friends but how many times in last few months you expressed it to them. How many times you sat close to your mother and said looking in her eyes "Mom I love you a lot". We think it looks awkward and she already knows it that I love her. But we fail to imagine the kind of joy and happiness we can give them by expressing. I remember one such instance, which makes me feel that how live expression is important.

"My friend who is originally from New Delhi is employed in Hyderabad as a software engineer. He has a busy schedule, works for 12 hours a day and talks to parents occasionally. He comes to Delhi couple of times in a year. One day his dad had a severe heart attack and died. He immediately rushed to Delhi by air and when entered the home, he could see dead body of his father kept on the floor. He threw his bags away and hugged his father's dead body and said "Dad I loved you so much."

Now my question is that how many time he expressed this fact to his dad when he was alive, he is yelling now when dad can't hear anymore.

We are blessed with so many sweet relations, let's start expressing our true feelings for them and make them feel an integral and important part of our life.

Firmly Affectionate

Many a time people ask me a problem of taking them for granted by their friends and closed ones. When you keep on giving and other keeps on getting gradually the second one will start taking you for granted. As I told you earlier, that relationship is made of giving and taking hence one way relationship can't last long.

When you see somebody taking you very easy you can be little firm but don't leave your affection. A relationship is a combination of firmness and affection. This can be very well applied in child-parent relationship and employer-employee relationships.

A very interesting story explains the concept very well:

In a small village there was a well and all villagers used to fetch water from that well only. Once a wild poisonous snake started living close to that well. Now whoever goes to well to fetch water is bitten by the snake and died. People stopped going to the well rather they had to go to the next village to get water. Once a saint visited the village and asked villagers if they have any problem. They shared their problem of not being able to fetch water due to dangerous snake living there. The saint assured villagers to get rid of their problem. Saint went to the well enchanted some mantras and snake came out. He asked snake "Why don't you leave this place and make life of these villagers hassle free?" Snake replied "I can leave this place after biting you i.e. you have to sacrifice your life." Saint further said "I don't mind sacrificing my life for these people, but how should I trust you? What if you don't fulfil your commitment?" After this discussion both saint and snake entered into an agreement under which snake got agreed to not to harm villagers for next six months and after six months saint agreed to sacrifice his life. The saint assured all the villagers that their problem is now resolved and they can go to well without any fear. Slowly and gradually villagers started going to the well and fetching water.

After six months the saint returned to the village to fulfil his part of the commitment. First he asked villagers whether snake harmed them or not. Villagers confirmed that snake has turned to be a good creature and very friendly to them. Saint moved close to the well and called the snake but he didn't come out. After lots of searching efforts he found the snake under a bush in a miserable condition. Saint asked the snake "Oh my god how you reached to this bad condition, your skin is torn and you are appearing to be in a dying situation, how did it happen?" Snake replied "It happened because of you only, you asked me to not to bite and harm anybody for six months. I stood by my promise but these people took me for granted. Children of the village used to play with me. They started treating me like a piece of rope, throwing here and there without having any fear."

Saint finally replied with smile on his face. "My dear, I asked you not to bite them but I never stopped you protecting yourself. You would have hissed at them just to protect yourself.

The snake was friendly with them and people started taking him for granted. He would have saved himself or his self pride by being little firm.

Winning the People – the Power of Empathy

It is only in hardships that true relations filter out from all the bunch of relations we pretend to possess. And it is only during tough times that we can easily knit a strong bond with people. You don't have to be a superman, who can solve everyone's problem, but you just need to be an understanding heart, a heart wherein somebody's pain gets a resting shade, a heart that receives everyone's pain as it is my own situation.

We have all experienced the truism that life doesn't always go quite as smoothly as we would like. And that sometimes the curveball's that life throws at us can be very, very stressful. When times get tough, our focus naturally turns inward, and it's not unusual for people during these periods to feel alone and besieged. It is at moments like these that we appreciate empathy the most. We don't necessarily want someone to solve our issues (although that would sometimes be nice), but it's nice to know that someone grasps the implications of our situation.

To have empathy with other people mean to let them know that you understand and care about what they're going through. When it comes to connecting with other people, there is no stronger message that you can send. One of the most powerful sentences you can have in your communications toolbox, in fact, is: "From what you've told me, I can understand why you're frustrated", It says to the person that you've taken the time to listen, and that you recognize their emotional state. You're not necessarily agreeing with them, you're just empathizing with them.

At a time when someone is feeling like the world is against them, it is a positive message that they will appreciate and remember for a long time.

"***People need you at your best when they are at their worst***"

Hence we find interpersonal skills are an art of cautious and calm mind to deal with delicate hearts with an objective to spread the genuine strands of relations. And then a single happy heart can multiply & spread happiness all over, and fears and tears get divided to an extent that they become negligible. It not only ensures you a steady growth rate but also helps your personality outshine. Ultimately synchronisation of your heart with everyone earns you professional & personal satisfaction.

☺ You are My Friend ☺

Standing by,
All the way.
Here to help you through your day.

Holding you up,
When you are weak,
Helping you find what it is you seek.

Catching your tears,
When you cry.
Pulling you through when the tide is high.

Just being there,
Through thick and thin,
All just to say, you are my friend.

- Brittani Kokko

11

The Hero of Life

Raj had been a good student in his childhood, very sincere during his academic life. No doubts he got selected in a very good firm during his campus recruitment and at a very high package. Thereafter he had been a committed employee. Overtimes were a routine for him. Bringing work to home had become a daily ritual. He was involved into his work to such an extent that gradually his health had started deteriorating. Fatigue & exertion had become his constant partners. And consequently he had started living a sick life.

Vicky was a wealthy man. He was a great businessman. He had the sharpest of the mind among his competitors and was considered to be a paradigm for the same. Every moment he spent was to grow further and expand his wealthy business to great heights. In this blind race for more & more wealth what was left behind was his family. Every time when Vicky was required to share the small happy moments with his family he was always occupied by his business dealings. For his family and near and dear ones he was not available due to his work priorities.

Shelly belongs to Delhi. She has been a success story at an early age. Brilliant schooling, best college education and thereafter MBA from a renowned college gave her a competitive advantage. She is presently working with an MNC in Bangalore as a consultant. Online working allows Shelly to work flexibly from home itself. Initially Shelly's family used to visit her every two months. But due to her hectic schedule Shelly could rarely spend quality time with her parents. Despite of the flexibility available to work from home, Shelly could not give time to her parents. She was physically in front of them but still mentally occupied by her work. Gradually the frequency of visiting Shelly got reduced. And now once in a blue moon whenever Shelly's parents visited her, she has not even a second to spare for them. It was a panicking situation for her parents.

Heena & Rahul got married couple of years back. Both of them are well-placed in big firms in Pune. Rahul works in a company that's 30 kms away from his residence in east whereas & Heena works in a firm 25 kms away from her residence in north-west direction. Right from 5 in the morning to 11 at night, it's a challenging and hectic day for both of them. Weekends become the sole points of finishing off pendency. Rarely can they afford some time to enrich their relation. All what remained to share in the relation is: time & work. They use to talk in terms of schedules, timetable and daily chores of running a home. And in case if one person's schedule gets distorted it becomes a reason for arguments between the two. With the passage of time, instead of strengthening the relation it became more rough and painful.

Thus the pain unavoidably is becoming a part of everyone's life. The thing to observe in all the above stated realities of life is: suffering!! The reason is that some phases of life getting more than required focus and the other being ignored for no reason. Each one of us is presently facing a similar situation in our life. Our balance is unknowingly imbalanced.

Imbalance & Balance

Present day life has grown very hectic. Day by day, time seems to shrink and areas of work seem to expand. In the fast moving life, there are many pressures that new-age couples have to deal with- running a home, doing daily chores like cooking/cleaning, raising children and handle the tight deadlines at work! Each one of us has plenty of aspirations, number of dreams, various obligations and other important tasks to do in the limited time span available to us. All aspirations fall in different directions and one can afford to move only in one direction at a time. Yet in order to excel on the platform of life; covering all the aspects, travelling all the directions is a must. If we can manage to create a balance in our life we can certainly draw more happiness and contentment out of it.

On giving it a deeper thought we realize that the real fight is between the personal & the professional role. In other words the fight can also be designated as family versus finance. The solution is not to pursue one and sacrifice one. Neither can one do justice by giving first half of life to finance and the next half to family or vice-versa. We have to carry both the aspects simultaneously without being imbalanced. And that is where the biggest challenge appears- balancing the two most demanding and dominant parts of our life. This is the major focal point of every person's life that decides the ultimate rate of success in one's life.

I would like to share one true incident from my own city Kota. A famous doctor couple was running a hospital in the city for almost 15 years. After so many sacrifices, hard work and perseverance they could establish themselves to a good level. They had a son who was sent to the best school of the town, he was tutored by best of the teachers personally but parents didn't have much time for him. Parents wanted him to be a doctor so that their empire can be further grown. After passing 12th standard exam the son appeared for medical entrance test for three consecutive years but could not get through. He was given best of the coaching but somehow nothing could work. Finally the doctor couple decided to send him to a reputed medical college in Bangalore, after paying a donation of Rs. 35 Lacs. Their son stayed in Bangalore for almost 5 years, completed his MBBS and spending another Rs.20-25 lacs in this process. After his becoming doctor parents wanted him to come back to Kota and take charge of the family run hospital. Surprisingly son opted to go abroad. This doctor couple created a big imbalance on family front and there was no emotional bonding with the child. They sacrificed 15 invaluable years of their life and piled up 50 lacs of rupees which was spent in one go. The huge infrastructure created by them is of no use as their only son is not with them. At this juncture they feel shattered and now they can't have it again what they have already lost, the time, the family, the pleasure, the money and even the health.

I don't call it a life unless it is perfectly balanced.

Role v/s Role

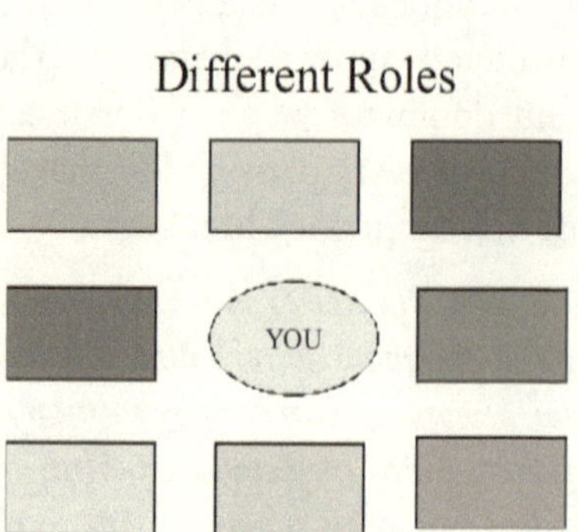

Everybody in this world has to play several roles in life. Broadly we have Family role, Role at business or work place, Role in the Society, Spiritual Role and Personal Role. Further In family we have different roles viz. Role of father/mother, Role of son/ daughter, Role of spouse and so on.

Let's identify the various roles you play in life presently:

You form the centre and the vacant boxes around you need to be filled with the variety of roles you play in your life. Like you may be an employee, a social worker, President of an association, active member of a professional association, a spouse, a father, a son, a brother, a good friend, a helping neighbour and so on. You may specify all the demanding roles of your life around you.

Thereafter the analysis process begins. You may use the following scale to rate the effectiveness of all the roles:

1 = Very Low Effectiveness

2 = Low Effectiveness

3 = Average Effectiveness

4 = Good Effectiveness

5 = Excellent Effectiveness

Out of all the roles stated in the periphery of you some roles would be more important and some roles may be nominal. Thus through this activity we are in a position to give a thought -which roles are we playing with full zest and which roles are still to be worked upon. The area of neglect that needs to be converted into the area of priority can be indentified through this figure. It enables you restore the balanced situation of your life. One needs to prioritize the roles of his life. It helps redirect life in alignment with one's dream vision. It would help you focus your efforts in the direction of the Mission of your life. Until and unless we identify our mission in life we will always stay puzzled in our lives doing unnecessary things.

The general overview we get through this activity is that in today's fast, competitive and mechanized environment everybody is focused towards one or few areas only, resulting into conflict in various roles played in life, neglect of some important areas and eventually creation of imbalance in life. That's why while making money people are prone to lose family happiness. Similarly, while focusing too much on social role one may lose his/her business growth. I have seen people highly focused on one or two things in their life that in longer course of time creates a big imbalance in life, causing lots of problems. I have seen people who are totally money oriented, totally spouse oriented, socially oriented and so on. But inclination only on one aspect for a longer time period seems to be detrimental to one's personal development and it handicaps the person's further growth. Therefore balancing all the roles & creating harmony between them is need of the hour.

Balancing it Perfectly

What are the key ingredients of a good life? In which parameters do we define an ideal living? There are multiple roles played by a single person daily, there are different people all around and a variety of situations to face, defining balance in a customized form is too tedious task to perform. So can there be a simpler way to understand the ruling factors of our life??

YES we do have a framework that encompasses every role of every person in every situation possible. This framework is defined as five F's of our life by US author Burke Hedges: Finance, family, fitness, and friends and last but not the least faith.

Drivers of Perfect Life Balance

Here are five important Balancing drivers of life:

Health: Well-stated Fact, Health is wealth!! I have seen people ignoring their health and running after success. When they think of taking the savour of success their health doesn't permit them. One of my clients had hectic working schedule, never put any efforts in systematic eating or physical workouts. He had his first heart attack at the age of 32 only. He has piled up billions in his bank accounts along with plenty of immovable properties but all this is value less amidst the fear of dying. Many of the billionaires can't eat sweets, can't eat butter or food of their choice, some of them feel tired with little exertion. Life seems hail when health doesn't support you and all our luxuries appears to be useless. We must invest in our health regularly before it starts giving you warning signals. Somebody has rightly said, "Disease is nothing but penalty of our negligence."

Family: It not only includes your family members but it denotes the emotional bonding that you share with them. It includes the aspects of mutual understanding, care and affection for the people who are a part of your family. And it is not by choice but by God's grace that you belong to particular family. This god-gifted plant needs immense care in terms of time, space & understanding then only it can serve as an evergreen shade for you. Else, instead of promoting our growth it may act in opposing direction thus creating an imbalance. We must learn spending quality time with our loved ones. If someone comes to know that he or she is going to live only for few days, suddenly their priorities will change and everyone would like to spend the remaining time with their loved ones. Our family members need us first and everything else is later.

Again all luxuries are useless if we don't share strong bonding and sweetness in the relations with our family members.

Money: Though we believe that money cannot buy us peace and happiness but still we need it as necessity of life. We have right to earn and spend. It brings quality to our life through good education, good medication and good living. Therefore a part of life or routine should be focused towards earning of that quality for you and your family members. But running blindly behind money and compromising with your health and family is going to create a heavy imbalance in your life.

At the end of the day no money, no business, no pleasure, no friends are that important as your own body, say as your own health. I have seen many people compromising to their health and then struggling badly in spite of having all luxuries at home. Some of them develop diseases like blood pressure and sugar at an early age. They can't eat freely and can't exert much. There is no life without good health. You need to maintain balance from the beginning. Once you lose fitness it's very difficult to restore it. Later on when time flies nothing remains except repenting upon what you have lost.

Colleagues & Friends: Friends fill in colours to our life, they add on more meaning to our life. A friend is an ultimate source of relief to everyone of us. Being in touch with friends helps making life more soothing. As no dish is complete without spices, no success can be enjoyed; no pain can be relieved without friends in life.

Faith & Self Satisfaction: Add all above components, and yet success seems to be impossible when trust on own self is absent. Faith in our own ability, our own skills is must to perform our best in life. Faith in god makes us a complete and contended person. We have seen people working for humanity or searching for the peace despite everything was available to them. Faith is one kind of self satisfaction which you attain when you do something what you love most, you do something for the society or you do something to fetch the innermost satisfaction.

Thus missing any of the drivers of life will make Life meaningless causing lots of imbalance. The balance of all the spices mentioned above is prerequisite to complete life properly. All five key areas cover the major aspects of our life. Despite of having this basic awareness about the significance of these factors, we tend to ignore these aspects very easily. Those who give appropriate focus to all the five key areas mentioned above get the maximum happiness out of their lives.

BE the Hero of Your Life

Practically speaking, maintaining such a balance seems to be next to impossible. Increasing work pressure, increased demanding relations and various personal needs somewhere or the other creates imbalance. The ideal situation demands a person to be a 'Perfect man'. A perfect man is one who can manage all the diverse aspects of life smoothly. One has to be a Hero in life. Hero means an all rounder who is master of every field and makes everybody happy and contended. Personal & professional life, both play a significant role to ensure quality life. One needs to take both the aspects together: work and life. More favouritism to any one of them leads to imbalance in life. Work and life are equally important for a man's sustained happiness and satisfaction.

Out of Balance.... Out of Control

Balance is an ideal situation, and having some amount of imbalance is inevitable. But letting the imbalance take dominance, makes it more and more uncontrollable for us. Imbalance state is created daily. But the same can be rectified, brought on track that too on daily basis. Its not only money that one needs, ultimately we all need time and peace.

Important vs. Urgent

Some things are important in life and some activities though not that very important but yet are necessary for our survival. Important things cannot be kept out of focus nor can we let go the necessary tasks unperformed. But this is a normal human behaviour to work in reverse mode. A student generally starts studying a month before his exam. A man pays the electricity bill in the last three days of the due date, all works are done in reverse time scheduling only. Such a working may not seem to be harmful. But we tend to wait for a normal activity to become an urgent one and thereafter come under compulsion to leave aside our other important task and finish off the urgencies first. This is where the imbalance distorts our normal working and puts us under tension or mental pressure.

Such people always seem to be in haste, in situation of crisis, and could not enjoy anything. Until and unless you switch over from doing urgent things you will never be in the position to do the important things of your life. We all wish to do big things, good things, and work that we enjoy, but rarely can we afford time to walk the path our way. Following measures may assist in switching over from urgent to important:

Plan Before Doing

Every day the path that you need to tread in next 24 hours should be mapped in your mind. It helps in quick decision making and attaining most of the targets of the day efficiently.

Carry a Note Book

To grow means to handle many things at a time. In such a hectic life it is natural to forget some things, miss out some important work and it seems impossible to rely 100% on our memory for perfect flawless working. A small notebook is the best tool to assist in this problematic situation. Always keep a pen & a small note book in hand. This is the first step to success. This gives a feel of your being ready to accept all tasks with 100% commitment to yourself. And it is this habit that helps you complete all the tasks without memory loss effect impacting you.

Concentrate

It is obvious when you are at work family matters may bother you, when you are in a party things relating to business may knock your thoughts again and again. This re-wandering of the thoughts reduces your efficiency at work. We must be in the position to first of all identify such disturbing thoughts, and then with strong will power such untimely links should be cut off so that we are in the position to focus on our present work. Its only through concentration that we can work with 100% efficiency and accomplish all our targets on time. Focused approach is must to give best results feasible.

Take Breaks:

Small breaks help us refresh our spirits, mind and body. That helps us charging our mind & body, so that we may get back to work with the same zeal.

Learn to Delegate Things

One of the most important rules of working is to delegate as much as possible. Delegating helps you get the work done quickly plus it helps you focus on the most important work of yours.

Don't Procrastinate

Procrastination in simple terms is delay without any genuine reason. In other words procrastination is an enemy of your success. The more you delay the farther your destination will be from you. Never let lethargic attitude dominate your work, and always stay proactive & vigilant.

Synchronizing

We enjoy the weather, if it synchronizes with our mood. If you have to attend a party today but you are feeling feverish, will you enjoy it? No, because your health is not in tune with the environment. When two people think in opposite directions, arguments are bound to be a part of their relation. Thus we observe that things in tuning are more pleasant and less of a torture for us. Nor two persons on this earth have 100% same living, neither they can have 100% same thinking. Even twins are never completely identical. Variations add on more beauty to this human world. It is through this wide variety only that we get to learn the amazing ways to live life. Opposite roles, different thoughts all are there to complete each other.

Everything is complementary in life: like joy & sorrow, profit & loss, friend and enemy – all elements of nature tend to balance our life: neither to make it too sweet nor to make it too sour, and yet it is not even tasteless. All the opposite elements make life spicier.

Working in present and thinking of past, living in present and mere dreaming of future – What would be the output of the day which is spent in either of the two ways? Certainly it would be Nil. Rather the output is not also zero, it goes in negative as we bear loss in terms of time, money and energy.

There are two eternities that can break you down: Yesterday & tomorrow. One is gone & the other one does not exist, so live in present. It's an art ot living in present. Reiterating past happenings, day dreaming of future planning will lead to no output. The best way to live today is to live in today only, not in past or future.

Quality Life

You are the director of your life. The role you play in life is chosen by you. The accomplishments and hallmarks you create are your own self created. You cry or you smile is your own choice. You yell out your pain or you silently absorb it – is again all your choice. You have the power to give meaning to your life- a meaning that is unique. A meaning that makes your life outshine as pearl. Just like a performer balances all the moves to give her best on the stage, similarly we need to balance all the aspects as beautifully as possible. The way roses are accompanied by thorns, without affecting its beauty, in the same manner the wide range of streams are connected to our lives simply to add on more meaning to it. If all the streams are well balanced, our life becomes more meaningful and beautiful.

We reach at such a level wherein we play all our roles to the fullest and do justice to everyone associated with us, thus enhancing the ultimate quality of our life & making it truly worth living.

Practical Balancing Formulae

Following actions will certainly help you creating a good balance in your life:

- Appreciate as much as possible.
- Spend at least 5 minutes talking to a friend. It helps relieve your daily tensions.
- Spend 20 minutes in light exercise/jog. It avoids strain from affecting our physical health.
- Do at least one pending task of yesterday. It helps reduce mental burden.
- Read 15 pages of non-fiction book. It helps refuel the internal flame.
- Spend one hour with your family. It helps walk on the concept of burden sharer and burden bearer.
- Spend 15 minutes with yourself. Give time to yourself. Renew the balanced thoughts of mind.
- Prepare to do list for tomorrow. Planning is the first step to achieve things in a systematic manner. Being proactive helps us predict & prepare accordingly for the next day.
- Control your temptations: extreme of anything and everything is harmful. A balanced state is not harmful. Getting tempted towards something leads to sheer imbalance. Strict self control can help out in it.

- Avoid bad habits: Avoid being used to the imbalance of life and getting addicted to mere temporary substitutes rather than permanent solutions. Most of the people working in call centre get so much stressed out due to their odd work schedules that slipping to such temporary relaxing pleasures like smoking, drinking seems to be an obvious solution. But the bare reality is that these temporary solutions ruin our live permanently.
- Live a life that has a beautiful rhythm, a life that does not become a burden, but flows like the pacifying river water. A life that does not seem as wood of dry trees, but appears to be a garden of flowers: flowers of different colours & fragrance ultimately adding more value to your life.

Manage Your Stress Effectively

Imbalances in life if not paid timely attention leads to dilution of quality of our lives. It makes us feel lost. We lose our social circle. We may lose our health, our mental peace. The world seems to be lonelier, when things begin to overwhelm you and the whole world seems hopelessly gray, the symptoms of stress start appearing within us. Stress is a phenomenon of feeling tired & feeling low and it can be termed as a kind of mental disease. Though a survey reveals that financial and relationship problems are two major reasons of stress across the world still there are few more reasons which cause stress:

Increasing Competition

Write from the school education to professional education, competitive entrance exams, getting a job, working in a company and managing own business everywhere the competition is getting stiffer day by day. We have no other option but to fight with these challenges but somewhere it is causing lot of stress to all of us.

Modernization & Urbanization

New technology, use of cell phones, and continuous connectivity with people online, working continuously in front of the laptop's screen, less of humane essence in vicinity complicates the situation more. Lot of traffic, daily commuting to work place, pollution etc. are all contributing to our stress tank silently.

Expectations

We all have varied expectations from our job, our family and with our own self. All these roles also have some expectations from us. For e.g. Say I decide to wake up at 4 am daily. But daily I end up breaking my own expectations by waking up at 6 am puts me under stress. It unknowingly deep inside generates a feeling of looser. When expectations are not fulfilled our mental toughness gets hammered. The more it shatters, the more we get prone to stress and to stress related diseases. My wife expects me to returned back home at 7 in the evening but I fail to fulfil this expectation amidst expectations by my profession. This all cause stress to both ends.

Jealousy, ego & Comparisons

It's a very simple concept of life, when you say you are unique then how can you compare yourself with anyone else. There is no other masterpiece as are you on the Earth. But this is where we fall very often in lives. Due to narrow scene in our minds we end up comparing ourselves with others. Ego and jealousy are biggest self created causes of stress.

Reaction

Life is one percent what happens and 99% how we react to it. Unnecessary over exaggerated reactions to an event can only lead to tensions and mental stress, for which no one else can be blamed.

Mismanagement of Time

Stress also comes up as a reason of poor time management. When we are not able to make our life fertile, it leads to self-annoyance, you feel so low, ultimately leading to unwanted virus called stress.

Limitation to Change

When due to some reasons flexibility is not possible and change cannot be accomplished, rigidity is encountered which leads to frustration. Those who are flexible and adapting to the situation very fast stay relaxed. But due to many limitations we resist changes and somewhere inside it create suffocation.

Relationship Problems

Personal and professional relations, if are not smooth, leads to undue stress in life.

Workplace Environment

The workplace environment, if not up to the expectations, leads towards dissatisfaction. You work, but you work for the sake of working, the zeal, the enthusiasm, that willing contribution to the organization fades away. Besides, your self-satisfaction level also suffers. Again & again you have to face the same question. Is this the direction I really want to move ahead in? This puzzled stage fuels in more stress into life.

Types of Stress: Avoidable & Unavoidable Stress

Studies say that two third of the stress people face in life is avoidable. Avoidable stress is created due to illusionary thinking, unnecessary flow of negative thoughts, jealousy, ego, comparisons. All these can be controlled, by keeping a continuous watch over our thoughts and exercising strict 'No entry' rules for thoughts that put us down.

Unavoidable stress is a part of our living. No one leads a life filled with roses. Some thorns are ought to come in this life and they cannot be avoided. But the unwanted, self created, pseudo stress has to be discharged.

Stress not only harms our CPU (brain), but also hampers our physical growth, impairs our social periphery, leads to emotional swings, and leads to spiritual diluteness.

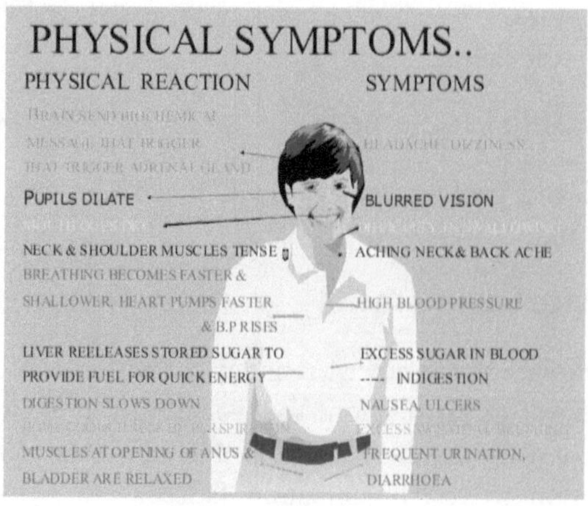

Symptoms of Stress

Physical symptoms of stress leads to High blood pressure, frequent cold, body pain, loss of sex drive, change in sleep pattern, migraine problems, frequent urination, shortness of breath and so on.

Mental symptoms of stress are: lapse of memory, poor concentration, confused state of mind, difficulty in making decisions, negative self talk, pessimism, poor judgment, suicidal thoughts, disorientation and panic attacks.

Emotional symptoms of stress: rapid mood swings, impatience, anxiety attacks, depression, worry, feeling of despair, burst of tears, nervous laughter, deterioration in personal hygiene and appearance.

Social symptoms of stress: preferring to stay aloof, loving loneliness, intolerance, lack of communication and avoiding group presence or public presence.

Results of Stress

Stress reflects itself in various forms. People lose confidence, appetite, sleep, mental peace, concentration, memory and good health. A stressful person feels as if his life has lost its meaning, there is no sense in living this hopeless life, despair flows in consistently, a feeling of emptiness generates. You tend to lose your temperament easily, less of forgiveness and patience is there. Life becomes directionless. You become more offensive, attacking and end up hurting every second person coming in your way. Such thoughts are self killing approach of a person, who exists physically but is dead inside. Existence of such a person leads to more of a depressing atmosphere all around. All what is required at such moment is complete change life by putting in the level best to pull yourself out of such a strenuous negative thinking and bringing yourself back to the brighter phase of life.

Getting Rid of Stress

Every cloud has a silver lining. Every problem has a solution and so has stress. Various techniques can help us be stress free. Few of the techniques are stated below:

Stop Thinking that what others think:

It's a simple fact, to live happily live as if you are the king or live as if you don't care who is the king? Live life with full zeal, fulfil your dreams, fill life with your own colours, your own contrasts, your own designs and make it a masterpiece to serve as a tribute to the Almighty who gifted you this beautiful life. Stop bothering yourself with other's thoughts. It's your life, you have every right to shape it as per your will and make your life a success story for the world to applaud.

Shout Like Children

It's a general tendency that many people suppress their pains deep inside. Make your heart as deep as ocean and as vast as sky. But when situation inflict on you, pain which is beyond your tolerance level, give it out to the sky. Shout out loud. This concept also flows in accordance with the natural law of give and take. When you came to this earth your heart was so cheerful. The pain you get on this earth has to be given back to world. But the best way to give it back is to give it no-one in personal, yet give it to entire world in general, so simply shout out loud in air.

Develop Productive Habits

Read books, learn music, play games, enjoy dancing, go for aerobics, join a gym, join some good association. Give your life more meaning and keep yourself occupied by such interests of yours that avoid stress from making an abode in your heart.

Find the Person to Share

Each one of us has a one close person, from whom we expect to understand us to the fullest with whom, we can share our feelings to the fullest. If you don't share what is bothering you, you will be more suffocated inside. The moment we feel bad we should share it with someone close to us, it really makes us feel light.

Meditation

It is a powerful way to control your thoughts. It helps you become more stable and mentally tough. It ensures 100% spiritual growth and hence helps you face difficult situations in life with ease.

Motivating Books and Friends

Keep oiling your lamp consistently to let the flame burn more brightly. A continuous flow of positivity serves as an antibiotic for your mind, and reiterates positivity in our mind. You must inculcate the habit of reading inspiring and motivating book. Keep in touch with friends who encourage you with their speech and behaviour.

Appreciate Yourself

No doubts we all have failed many times in life, but not every time. There are successful moments as well.

No doubt we all have some lapses, some flaws in us, but yet we are not totally unproductive. Each one of us has his or her share of appraisals, worthy talents and skills that are rare to find in others. So are we not worth appreciation? Self appraise helps us restore balance and faith in our self in tough times.

Have Faith in God

God can do miracles. Impossible can be made possible. Every situation, every moment has to pass by. No pain, no joy nothing is going to stay forever. Have faith in God. This faith may not alter the present situation suddenly but will give the inner strength to bear that situation till it passes by.

Use Roll Back Technique

Think of the ultimate situation when you are having some tension. Try to visualize the worst and prepare yourself mentally to that situation. If you are ready to face the worst then you will not be scared. Then start thinking and acting how you can make the outcome better. Say if I have fear of decline in my business resulting in huge losses, first perceive a situation that everything has lost and you are accepting the situation. Once you are cool with the possible outcome then start thinking how you can improve the outcome. In this situation you stop thinking negative and whole of your energy is used in positive thinking and constructive acts.

Laugh as Much as You Can

Ultimately we live to be happy and cheer up everyone who comes in our touch. Laugh out loud. Cheer up, enjoy and let all the stress be released out of your heart.

Other Measures

Sleep well and don't sacrifice your sleep at the cost of worldly tensions. Have a proper diet, if possible a proper diet chart, with fixed timetable of intakes. One needs to exercise regularly to let traces of oxygen revive your entire nervous system thoroughly. Fresh eatables and freshness of body rejuvenates life and charges you up with more vibrant energy particles.

No one can touch your interiors without your permission. No one can divert you until and unless you want, no one can defeat you until and unless you let someone lead you. Self power is the most dominant force existing on this earth. Self instructions & consistent control help ensure balance in life. It is must to give some space and time to your own self to renew the balancing situation. Give relaxing time to yourself.

A healthy social network goes a long way to de-stress you and bring you to sparkling state again. Games, caring agencies, self help groups, religious organizations, media and all go a long way to help people come out of stress and resume the balance of their life.

Control Your Anger, Before it Controls You

"Anger is an acid that can do more harm to the vessel in which it is stored than to anything on which it is poured."

- Mark Twain

Do you ever find yourself getting more and more angry and frustrated while trying to explain what is bothering you? Perhaps you feel like others are not really listening to you or trying to understand things from your perspective. In such circumstances, you may end up raising your voice or becoming verbally or even physically abusive. Unfortunately, responding in this manner usually decreases your chances of being listened to with empathy and compassion.

Anger causes us damages from all corners. It increases the stress level, pulls down our efficiency and we lose control over ourselves. Your relationships are affected badly by your anger. Someone says that each one of us has an animal instinct inside us. The moment we get angry the animal inside us takes the control on our mind. That's why I have seen many educated and cultured persons shouting or fighting in public for silly reasons. It really hurts our image. People keep distance from those who are habitual of getting angry. What I personally feel, anger is very momentary and if you are able to hold yourself back for few seconds in hot times you can abstain from getting angry. If somebody annoys you and you feel like shouting or slapping him, stay calm for 10 seconds and you won't feel like doing it now.

Tips to control Anger

1. **Try counting to ten or think before saying anything:** This may not address the anger directly, but it can minimize the damage you will do while angry. Ultimately you want to get the work done or seek information from peers or your team. Anger is not the solution and spoils the way if any to complete the task.

2. **Learn to relax:** This is easier said than done some times, but if you find something that calms you it is a good way to keep your anger under control and a good way to maintain a calm environment in such situation.

3. **Laugh it off:** Think of something funny and laugh out loud. It is very difficult to be angry when you are laughing.
4. Step and think before you speak and leave any sarcasm out of the conversation.

Heal Yourself

The moments of Happiness Are part of our life
Shared by moments of misery
Making it difficult to strive sometimes we may fail
Some sighs and regrets
But by constantly trying, our goals are met
Going through a Failure is an era
of profound grief, But each experience in life
Has something to teach
The woe and tribulation, the pain and sorrow
These are our own
With no one to borrow, be an optimist and
Accept your defeat
Life is very abundant, take it as a treat
So let's be merry and start with
A new day, the troubles are small pebbles
To be kicked away!
(Composed by Pritam Kumar Goswami)

12

THE SOUL

(Values, Ethics & Social Concerns)

Values

Simplest of all, values are the foundation of our life. Your definition of right or wrong, your justification for your decisions & actions is termed as values. The beliefs, the norms that we hold for others, for our life, for our living are termed as values. They serve as the base which helps us decide what is right and what is wrong. It is a personal sense of right and wrong. The basic mental ideology that helps us decide our course of action, that helps us define our life, that helps justify the difference of right and wrong is values. Values shape our character.

Values- Your Foundation of Life

Values keeps a person strong from inside, when you are correct and justified you feel self satisfied and that boosts up your inner strength. Values strengthen our moves ahead in life. Just recall the moment when you last praised anyone, what is the immediate effect? You feel good. You earn self satisfaction. You displayed the value of appreciation. Ultimately incorporation of human values in our lives gives mental toughness, mental peace & satisfaction.

It decides our attitude in life: Our attitude, our lifestyle, our adaptability & our actions all are determined by our value system. A strong value system ensures right attitude & right behaviour towards things.

Values help in sound decision making: It serves as the framework that provides significant focal of taking correct decisions apt according to the existing situation. Strong value system helps take proper decisions without any delay or confusion.

Values ensure perpetual existence: Winning the game is not that difficult but playing the game without breaking the rules matters. Short term success without strong value system can be easily achieved, maintaining the same in future becomes a challenge.

Contributes to your brand image/ helps you become a role model: The easiest thing to change in this world is you. To groom your organization or your children one has to be ethical first. Be a role model and serve as an example for the world. Let the world follow you. Enhance your brand value.

Types of Values

General natural laws that define the human conduct on earth are known as the universal values. The values exercised without geographical boundaries, separation of caste & creed like loyalty, humility, helpfulness applies all over the world without discrimination.

Man made values are the beliefs developed based on our religion, our locality, our background and the upbringing. These values are self-created beliefs of individuals or a group of people.

A girl belonging to a family living in village has numerous restrictions on her. Without permission she is not allowed to even step out of the house, her dressing is so restricted etc. Right from childhood she is kept as if she is meant only for kitchen and domestic work as if by birth she is devoid of talents & natural skills.

The same family when moves to a town, the scene changes. The girl child is given a bit of freedom, she is given her right to education & her right to make friends and still this right comes secondary to her home- responsibilities. Some freedom is granted to her as per the region and environment around.

Now if the same family resides in a city, again a new scene can be observed. Now she has right to complete her education, move out with friends, wear western outfits and she can actually explore her talents with much liberty.

Let's move on to a metro now, now the angel has no more restrictions in mind, neither does the family bother that much. As per the normal culture she is free to enjoy late night parties, go to discs, and flaunt latest attires. She is free from botheration completely in such a scenario.

Let's make a move to London now, the family readily adapts to the prevalent customs. Who cares even if you go and have a stay out for a couple of days? Live in relation sounds much normal there. The way they justify their actions are the set moral standards of that place.

By the mere shift of the family the way a girl is allowed to spend her life changes drastically. The rules of the region dominate the liberty level in her life. I do not say that live in relation is good or bad, the point brought to the limelight is that the self created norms change the way we live. It depends from society to society, religion to religion, status to status and region to region. Such values that change based on such demarcations are man-made values. But the values that trespass these boundaries and apply universally to every individual on this earth are the universal laws of nature.

Not to ditch anyone is an implied value. To stay true to your family, your spouse is a universal value. Never hurt anyone is natural belief. Such values are not bound by our religion, our locality, our status, our nationality. They are the natural human aspects which everyone living on this earth has to embrace to ensure a better living.

Competence & Character

What is more important in a person: his competence or his character?

Let's imagine four different combinations in a person:

Competence: Low	Character: Weak
Competence: High	Character: Weak
Competence: Low	Character: Strong
Competence: High	Character: Strong

The first and the last states can be easily identified and the general social norms for the same are also clearly stated by law. The dilemma arises when one has to choose between state II & state III. Let's talk about a doctor. The degree is earned by real hard efforts, and the profession even makes it a compulsion for the doctors to take the Hippocratic oath to promise not to misuse their knowledge and exploit the ignorant people of the society. Yet the newspapers reveal the cases like body organs stolen, body parts for sale, Doctors operating on a dead body only due to the lucrative commercial aspect etc.

A person with best of the best knowledge & degrees may earn money but not respect, he may earn wealth but not worth, he may earn luxuries but not purity.

Knowledge may be valued but a person short of character cannot be accepted by the society.

A person with no knowledge, but strong character may not be successful, may not lead an extraordinary life, but can win hearts, can win trust, can earn peace but certainly not going to be an achiever or role model for people.

Thus to be an outstanding person in both 'Sound Character' and 'High Competence' are required.

Hence to be successful, the base is your character and the knowledge & competence act as the pillars. If the base is strong tall pillars can be constructed but if the base is weak no pillars can stand for long on it. Both the ingredients are necessary to ensure a sound growth in life.

Implementing the beliefs within different peripheries:

Three different peripheries of ethical moves are generally known as under stated:

1. Personal values
2. Social values
3. Business Values

Personal values: Once I went to the market. It's my normal tendency to park my car in the right parking lot. But due to some urgency I parked my car right in front of the store from where I had to do the purchasing. Immediately the traffic police appeared and pointed out my wrongly parked car. I rushed out to rescue my car when the DSP walked out and questioned me about my profession! I stated I am a chartered accountant just to hear the sheer remark: '*if educated people like you would break rules like this, what can we expect from those who are illiterate?*', That day I came to know that when we practice values there is no room for error. You can't take excuse that others are also doing wrong or you have been doing things right but by chance you did wrong this time. You are being watched and noticed constantly by son many eyes.

Values of every individual, individual choices, thinking & reasoning are a part of personal values. Personal values depend on the individual. They may not be same for two different persons. What is correct according to me, may not fit in your domain of goodness. Every person has different mindset, different preset norms, habits & ideology that guide their complete conduct. It is these set of norms that are specific to a person and are termed as personal values.

For example a person who is punctual will always be punctual no matter whether he is in New Delhi or New York? A person who is honest will always stay honest no matter how people prefer to grow & no matter even if honesty is visibly not given importance. The character that you wear is going to enhance your own brand value. No one else can neither be benefitted nor will have to bear a loss due to your personal values. Your beliefs are going to define your own conduct, your decision making & are going to justify your own behaviour in this world. Pick up any person on this earth who has earned success, and analyze what is the cause behind it- you take Amitabh Bachhan- observe how many times does he blink his eyes in a minute?? Observe the level of focus with which he works? It is just the visible impact of his invisible personal value of focus, deep concentration & power to cut off diversions.

We all have heard a lot about N R Narayan Murthy!! A great corporate leader indeed! What is his unique quality? No doubts, he is a sharp minded person like other world class leaders of India, yet something unique about this man can be found in his biography- that's his simplicity !!

I am sure each one of us knows the proverb: Simple living, high thinking! Dear friends, what we all know as a fact, is actually put to work by this person and this is from where he earns his success.

Your personal values are your inner strength, your power booster and it is because of them that one can make impossible, possible! Nothing can stay for long, every success fades out, if it is not based on the firm base of humanity & until it lies on the strong foundation of personal ethics.

Today it doesn't matter that 'what' you are, rather 'Who' you are matters first!! So many people become doctors, but are all of them equally successful?? Why is that we find ourselves comfortable with only a handful of doctors? What is that difference in their conduct that goes beyond their professional degrees? All the Chartered Accountants hold the same degree still we are very selective and not everyone suits our preference and need? Why is it so, that we prefer going to a particular saloon only, when we know it may not be the best in the corner? It's all because there is something beyond the professional service we receive from them. It is about the trust, the comfort, the feeling of warmth we get from that place. It is the blind faith we develop for that particular person in that profession, that despite of being aware of the best performers in that field we still keep our self restricted to our regular service provider.

Tell me one thing, whenever you hurt a person, how do you feel? Whenever you say a lie to your boss to take a leave, does for that time period your heart starts beating at a faster pace? Whenever we park our cars on the wrong side, don't we keep on checking from the store itself, is it okay?? Whenever we scold our subordinate badly we feel uneasy, why? There are various moments when we do things and it hurts us only, but why??

The answer is simple- we go against our own set of rules of life; we fail to follow the natural laws of nature. It's not that we are not aware of the personal values, the natural norms of human conduct, yet in our normal course of life we tend to overlook them, we unknowingly get situation-stuck and the moment we go against the norms set deeply in our own heart, it hurts. Success never materializes, like this.

It is easy to dilute our quality looking at the surrounding we belong to, it is very easy to slip down saying 'that is how the world walks', it is simple to wear off your values stating that nobody cares in present world; but what is important is that, those who are successful are still holding their personal values with them. Mixing yourself in the crowd is easy, and seems to be a simple solution in tough times, but what is demanding is to withhold your values too, and no matter what never let it dilute, never let your shine be vanished by the storm, Its only these values that make you a gem and differentiate from the rest of the world. To fetch a degree is not a big deal today, but to fetch a character is!!! To stick to personal values is a bigger challenge than gaining knowledge.

Always remember,

If you can't be a pine on the top of the hill
Be a scrub in the valley--but be
The best little scrub by the side of the rill;
Be a bush if you can't be a tree.

If you can't be a bush be a bit of the grass,
And some highway some happier make;
If you can't be a muskie then just be a bass--
But the liveliest bass in the lake!

We can't all be captains, we've got to be crew,
There's something for all of us here.
There's big work to do and there's lesser to do,
And the task we must do is the near.

If you can't be a highway then just be a trail,
If you can't be the sun be a star;
It isn't by size that you win or you fail--
Be the best of whatever you are!

- Douglas Malloch

Social Values

Values that are utmost necessary for the survival, for the growth and wellbeing of the society are the social values. Getting beyond the self mindset to a broader periphery, moving a mile ahead to serve the society comes into social value.

It is a well known fact that we get to learn so many things from the society; our very existence would become impossible without society. Life is good because of this environment, because of the human element in it and it helps us make our lives smoother and much better. Thus it becomes an implied responsibility of everyone to contribute to the well being of the society. The problem arises here itself. When it is stated it is the responsibility of 'everyone' we interpret it as 'everyone except me' .For e.g. If the power of the entire locality goes off, we can immediately get the matter resolved by calling the electrician or any help from electricity board persons. And so can everyone in the society do. It is this reliance that makes us lethargic. We happily relieve ourselves from our responsibility by assuming that the other people could do the needful too. And what if every single person starts thinking in the same fashion? It would take not even a day to doom down life and society as a whole. Living for self is easy, but living for everyone needs guts. What is the meaning of you and me being literate, well-educated and qualified, when we cannot adopt a civilized conduct? Who is responsible for the society- only you, or only me?? Who owes to the society? Is it only those some people of the government who are responsible to run this nation so and so?? Each of us owes to this society. We all are collectively and individually responsible for the pathetic state of our nation at large.

Active Citizenship in Japan

I had opportunities to travel Japan twice and spent almost 14 days in Tokyo, Osaka and Nagano. It was life time experience for me. Let me share few highlights with you.

We understand that Japan being a developed country is having best and advance infrastructure but I was indeed impressed with the attitude, behavior and mind set of Japanese. They are very patient yet very energetic and proactive. They are very polite and humble. You ask for any help even a stranger will help you beyond your expectations. If you take favor from someone, that person will say thanks before you express the gratitude. If you are boarding a bus, the driver wishes every one with lots of warmth.

If they can't help you due to some regulatory issue, they will convince you and lovingly deny with clear reasoning. E.g. we went to a blood bank to donate the blood but after consulting their regulations they gently refused as they can't take blood of a person who is living in India for more than 3 years. But with all respect we were allowed to have visit in the whole blood bank. Remember we went there like a complete strangers.

I found Japanese to be very quiet and focused. They talk only when it's needed. Like in a crowded metro train in Tokyo I witnessed pin drop silence which is amazing. Most interesting part is that at least half of them were reading a book in train whether sitting or standing. Next day morning around 9 when thousands of people change their train at Tokyo main station, I could only hear the noise of Sandals and shoes.

Whenever you meet Japanese people, they welcome you with hundred percent genuine smile on their faces. They trust people a lot and never doubt anybody's intention.

Japan is known for its punctuality. Even if you observe smallest of the person or event you will find that people maintain their schedule minute by minute. Like for Conference we used to board shuttle buses. If the shuttle bus is to start at 4 PM it will not delay by even 30 seconds. That's amazing.

I saw that most of the working people wear black suite irrespective of his/her position or designation. They seem to be complete professionals. Many people use bicycles there for short distance drives. Even a person going to office in coat suite rides a bicycle. Their concern for environment protection is awesome. People are so much accustomed with rules that you can never see somebody violating the rule. If you move on the roads you hardly hear any horn. Two vehicles keep a distance of 8-10 feet, even on the traffic signal. They have high tech taxis and taxi drivers are thorough gentlemen. They wear tie and formals.

You can't see people talking rudely, showing arrogance, speaking in high pitch and fighting with each other. Even if there is some collision on the road (which is in fact very rare), you will see person coming out of the car shaking hand with other person having look at the damaged car and going back with a smile on the face. They have such an atmosphere that you stay afresh even in the evening, you really don't feel tired. Pollution level is very low.

How is it possible for Japanese to work with such efficiency, to always stay cool and calm, despite of the fact that we all face similar situations with similar troubles? Yet their reaction to it is so different. It's truly amazing!!

In spite of so many challenges and climatic adversities, what Japan is today, it is not only because of its government, but because of every single person, Who's life is a perfect paradigm of well defined social values. It is not the nation; it is the people of the nation who are responsible for its growth.

Words of A P J Abdul Kalam

Former president of India Dr. APJ Abdul Kalam is a living legend and inspires many. His vision for civilized India is something which forces every Indian citizen to think. I received an e mail from my friend with a strong message by Dr. Kalam to an Indian citizen. It goes like this:

I was in Hyderabad when a 14yr old girl asked me for my autograph. I asked her what her goal in life is. She replied: I want to live in a developed India. You must proclaim India is not an under-developed nation; it is a highly developed nation.

- YOU say that your government is inefficient.

- YOU say that our LAWS are too old.
- YOU say that the municipality does not pick up the garbage.
- YOU say that the phones do not work; the railways are a joke, the airlines is the worst in the world, mails never reach there destination.
- YOU say that our country has been fed to dogs and is the absolute pits.
- YOU Say, say and say. What do YOU do about it? Take a person on his way to Singapore. Give him a name ….YOURS. Give him a face….. YOURS.
- YOU walk out of the airport and you are at your international best. – In Singapore you don't throw cigarette butts on the road or eat in the stores.
- YOU are proud of their Underground Links as they are.
- You pay $5 to drive through road (equivalent to Mahim causeway or Pedder road) between 5PM and 8PM.
- You come back to the parking lot to punch your parking ticket if you have overstayed, identity. In Singapore you don't say anything, DO YOU?
- You wouldn't dare to eat in public during Ramadan, in Dubai.
- You would not dare to go out without your head covered in Jeddah.
- YOU would not dare to buy an employee of the telephone exchange in London at 10 pounds a

month to, "see to it that my STD & ISD calls are billed to someone else."

- YOU would not dare to speed beyond 55mph (88km/h) in Washington & then tell the traffic cop "Jaanta hai mai kaun hun (Do you know Who I am?). I am so & so's son.
- YOU wouldn't chuck an empty coconut shell anywhere other than the garbage container on the beaches of Australia & New Zealand. Why don't you spit pan or tobacco on the streets of Tokyo? Why don't you use examination jockeys or buy fake certificates in Boston???? We are still talking of the same YOU.
- YOU can respect and conform to a foreign system in foreign countries but cannot in your own. YOU throw papers and cigarettes on the road the moment you touch the Indian ground. If you can be an involved and appreciative citizen in an alien country, why cannot you be the same here in India?
- Once in an interview the famous Ex-municipal Commissioner of Bombay, Mr. Tinaikar had a point to make. Rich people's dogs are walked on the streets to leave their affluent droppings all over the place," he said. "And then the same people turn around to criticize and blame the authorities for inefficiency a dirty pavements. What do expect the officers to do? Go down with a broom every time the dogs feel the pressure in his bowels?
- In America every dog owner has to clean up after his dog has done the job. Same in Japan. Will the Indian citizens do that here?" He's right.

We go to the polls to choose a government and after that forfeit all responsibility. We sit back wanting to be pampered and expect the government to do everything for us whilst our contribution is totally negative. We expect the government to clean up but we are not going to stop chucking garbage all over the place nor are we going to stop to pickup a stray piece of paper and throw it in the bin. We expect the railways to provide clean bathrooms but we are not going to learn the proper use of bathrooms.

- We want Indian airlines and air India to provide the best of the food and toiletries but we are not going to stop pilfering at the least opportunity. This applies even to the staff, that is known not to pass on the service to the public. When it comes to burning social issues like those related to women, dowry, girl child and others, we make loud drawing room protestations and continue to do the reverse at home. Our excuse? "It's the whole system which has to change, how will it matter if I alone forego my son's rights to dowry.
- "So who's going to change the system? What does a system consist of? Very conveniently for us it consists of our neighbours, other households, other cities, other communities and the government. But definitely not me and YOU. When it comes to us actually making a positive contribution to the system we lock ourselves along with our families into a safe cocoon and look into the distance at countries far away and wait for a Mr. Clean to come along & work miracles for us with a majestic sweep of his hand or we leave the country and run away.

- Like lazy cowards hounded by our fears we run to America to bask in their glory and praise their system. - When New York becomes insecure we run to England.
- When England experiences unemployment, we take the next flight out to the Gulf. - When the Gulf is war struck, we demand to be rescued and brought home by the Indian government. Everybody is out to abuse and rape the country. Nobody thinks of feeding the system. Our conscience is mortgaged to money.
- Dear Indians, the article is highly thought inductive, calls for a great deal of introspection and pricks one's conscience too?..
- I am echoing J.F. Kennedy's words to his fellow American to relate to Indians?. "ASK WHAT WE CAN DO FOR INDIA AND DO WHAT HAS TO BE DONE TO MAKE INDIA WHAT AMERICA AND OTHER WESTERN COUNTRIES ARE TODAY" Let's do what India needs from us.

Thank You, Dr. Abdul Kalaam

Thus, to truly gain the ownership of this nation, we all need to be a good citizen first. Its only when I work with such words "I am a responsible citizen of my nation", can I ensure national growth. Don't be a problem, but be a part of the solution. Be a contributor in positive sense to the nation, so that your presence may serve as an asset for your nation. That is where your true social values become active to the fullest.

Business Values

When you work on the corporate platform, rules of the game change. The personal values & social values seem to be out of scene then. Various dominant forces come into play and diverging from the general values becomes quite obvious.

The standards & norms applicable to the business arena come into the domain of Business values. Practically speaking to professionalize the corporate world various codes of conduct, guidelines, Rules & regulations are formulated by firms and industries & their implementation is assured through a proper control mechanism. Yet, the corporate world comes across numerous situations of ethical dilemma.

Satyam is a live example of trespassing ethical borders of business. Despite of all moral standards set, despite of the strict vigilance in professional terms, blunders did happen. The main motive of business is to earn profit. So a company may attain profits by any means. In case of Satyam false entries had been shown in the book of accounts of the company. Such a deceiving act on the part of a global level company shattered the trust of millions of investors. The entire market got affected by such misconduct. Even worse, the deeper impact of the situation had to be borne by the Indian firms who are today seen with suspicion by the world. It's defamation at a huge level.

Another very obvious example seen in most of the firms is the selection, recruitment, promotion, transfer and all such employee related issues. Preset procedures are available with almost every company on all such aspects, yet references, biasness & discrimination play active role!!! Discrimination & harassment are the normal viruses found in most of the organizations by default. Employee welfare, employee are assets-are the theoretical concepts finding nominal space in practical world.

What should be your stand in such a situation? How can you assure ethical move in such a zigzag corporate world?

Guidelines for ethical business conduct:

Be your own Guide: Values are a powerful determinant of human accomplishments. It is the single key in the success of every individual. No matter what organization & workplace you are in, set your own personal and professional standards to abide by.

Keep your own moral thermometer on: Set your own personal values aside. Anything you do thereafter can be scaled with reference the ethical thermometer of your personal values. A reality check helps you taking correct moves neither, thus compromising with performance nor compromising with your intrinsic values.

Take ownership & responsibility: Let's say if your personal values are set right and whatever you do is as per your moral thermometer within the levels of ethical conduct. But what if something wrong happens in front of you? Had you been absent in that situation it would have been ok, but you being a witness of an unethical conduct, again puts you in dilemma of Right vs. Wrong !! Take the ownership and at least make sure no one is deceived in your presence, no one is hurt or cheated in your presence. Remember, being physically present in such a situation bestows upon you the implied responsibility of ethical behaviour.

Chose moral values over monetary values: Focus not on the monetary targets, but check the methods of achieving those targets. To earn good is not a big deal, but to earn ethically is a challenge.

Idealistic vs. practical: At times to fetch business deals, you have to go to great extent to make the client happy;

you have to go against your personal values. The self does not agree to move on with the organizational concept. Yet an employee is bound to follow the direction blindly.

Not every time ethics seems to be applicable. At times you ought to surrender due to your business obligations, to meet your monthly targets, to face situations which bound you to go against your personal values. It is obvious that you surrender, but all you need to assure is, never let your self become ethically low so easily. Keep up your ethical stand to the maximum extent possible. Let your ethical self be so strong that not so easily anyone can pierce it.

Openly discuss the issue: Whenever you have value conflicts. You could not justify some acts, discuss. Discuss with your friends, your colleagues, your superiors. Place forward the conflicting state that you observe. It will of a great way to solve your conflict. Justifications from the company help us align our value system with that of the firm, thus ensuring conflict free performance.

Values shape your character:

"Character is not reflected by what we say,
or even by what we intend,

it is a reflection of what we do." – Anonymous

"We are what and how we do,

Not what and how we idealize."

Character defines, builds or destroys your reputation. The consistency between what you say & what you do is Character. Values that you hold near to your heart shape your character. A strong character needs a firm value based system in life. No empire can be built on unethical foundation. Anything against human principles cannot survive.

Character is ultimately what you do, and whatever you do is based on the values you follow in life. Remember, once a wrong done, it gets sealed on your character. Whatever you do on this earth cannot be undone. No matter what your intentions were, what you actually follow and all excuses go in vain. One can never walk on the success-way with a weak value system. For success a strong value based conduct is utmost important. To be in the race for long, be morally strong. With a wrong mindset, no self confidence can be generated. In such a state even attitude seems to be arrogance. Dreams & vision lose their direction and things go against us. The very character that gets associated to our name stinks decline.

Values form the base of long term success!!

Service Above Self

We as a human being have an instinct to serve the humanity. In spite of inner desire to serve to the needy people many of us are not able to do do it because of some or other reason. I have seen many people living for others and serving unconditionally. We get so much from the nature, country, people and society but very few of us think of returning it back. Let's take a pledge and do something constructive for the society.

I have read about many such heroes who served above themselves. I want you to know few of them.

Dhaniram Panther

A great person with big heart, Dhaniram Panther of Kanpur, in last two years he has done cremation of more than 1350 unclaimed dead bodies. Once he saw police carrying two dead bodies on a cart in a miserable condition, it blew over his mind and since then he dedicated himself to this noble cause. His day starts with counting unclaimed dead bodies kept in mortuary and ends with cremation of all. He wants to spread his activity to whole of the state so that unclaimed bodies can be buried respectfully with dignity to their souls.

Mohd. Shareef

Untimely demise of his son changed his mind. He started living for others. He runs a small cycle repair shop in Faizabad, Uttar Pradesh. Whatever he earns across the day spends on poor and needy people. He gets up early in the morning and goes to any hospital of the city. He helps patients in bathing, gives them medicines, food and serves them as a family member. Patients call him "Shareef Chacha (uncle). He has become part of many hospitals and very popular among needy people. He visits hospital before opening the shop and after closing the shop. For his self less service he has been awarded "Godfrey Phillips Bravery Award".

Dr. Anuradha Sharma

Dr. Anuradha Sharma is running a school in Punjab in the name of "Hamari Kaksha" (Our Class) for very poor students where parents can't afford education for their children. She is funding the school at her own. Presently 1200 students are taking education in that school.

Sadhvi Ritambhara

Some political parties call her non secular, but she doesn't bother. Her mission is to bring a positive difference to society. She is famous as "Didi Maa" (Sister-Mother). She is running an orphanage cum school in the name of "Vatsalya Gram" in Vrindavan, Uttar Pradesh and hundreds of Orphan kids are being nurtured therein.

Just give it a thought. Are we paying back to the society or our country? Or we want to receive only. If we want to be the receiver, we have no right to curse the systems. Let's be the part of solution not the problem. Let's become the pioneer in making our society a nice place to live.

13

Learn from Legends

The world is full of passionate and enthusiastic people. Many people in this world despite all odds, physical challenges and family problems made those big problems look tiny. They touched pinnacles and reached amazing heights of life where a normal human being can't even think of. There are stories of many such people whom we call legends, which inspire us to do better in our lives. I have compiled few glimpses of some legends, who challenged the challenges thrown by life.

Jobby Changed his Destiny

Jobby Mathews from Kerala was sent to handicapped mercy home at an early age because he was too small and both his legs remained undeveloped. But he never wanted to be at somebody's mercy. At 12 years of age he topped in National Art Meet, New Delhi. Later on he wanted to be an athlete. In 1994 he won first national medal in arm wrestling. In 2005 in a world championship in Japan, he won three medals. In 2009 he won two silver medals in general and handicapped category in Egypt. He has won medals in 29th Arm Wrestling Championship in 2008 in Spain. He aspires to conquer the Mt. Everest too. He has proved that physical limitation no more a limitation unless that limitation is there in your mind.

A Visionary without Eyes

Mr. Charu Dutta Jadhav from Mumbai lost vision of his one eye when he was 13, and soon other eye too turned to blindness due to retina problem. He got lots of treatment but situation remained the same. He finished his graduation. Later on when he met so many such people in a camp of National association for blinds, he was inspired like anything. He got a bank job. He left that job and did MCA, MBA and advance certification course in Software programming and network security. Presently he is working with Tata consultancy services as an advisor. He has many achievements to his credit which physically capable people may not have. He is founder chairman of All India Chess Federation for Blinds. He is working on a technique to help blinds in education and jobs. In 2006 he was awarded by the president of India Mr. APJ Abdul Kalam for being Best handicapped workman.

One leg, No Problem

Girish Sharma of Rajasthan lost his right leg in a train accident when he was just two year old. Today he is 25 year old guy and a terrific badminton player. People get amazed seeing him playing flawless badminton on his left leg. He started his career as professional badminton player in 2005. Since 2008 he has been winning gold medals in National Paralympics in single and double championships. He was runners up in world championship in 2007 in Israel and won gold medal in Asian Championship in Bangalore.

No Arms & Legs! No Problem!!!

Philip Croijohn: in 1994 while adjusting his TV antenna he got a strong electric shock, doctors had to cut his legs and arms to save him. But he was not ready to compromise to his life. This 42 years French person is an accomplished swimmer and has crossed the English Channel in just 13.5 hours.

Nick Viyujik "The Miracle Man

He was born on 4th Dec 1982 in a Christian family. Generally people are happy and they celebrate the birth of a boy child. Both his parents and the doctors were shocked to see that he didn't have either of his hands and legs. They thought that the child will not be able to live for long but reports said that he was perfectly fine. But perhaps changing the fate was not in the hands of his mother so she inspired him to lead life courageously.

He started going to school but to attend the school with physically normal students was a challenge in itself; but his mother said that 'god has sent you on this earth for some special purpose, so don't ever lose your heart in extreme difficulties'. Since he was not capable enough to do physical exercise so he gave most priority to academic performance. Some years later he realized that people get inspired from him and in the way he speaks so after knowing his esteem potential in it he started motivational speaking.

One of his best books is 'No Arms, No Legs, No Worries' which give people a way to lead a happy living. Now he is self independent by investing in real estate. He has found that the will and dream to achieve something comes true one day, the God just makes us wait for the right time. God gives you strength to have Faith and hope in him and he is a live example of it.

Bobby Martin

Jersey numbered 99, I'm known by this name. I'm one and the only fast forward footballer in the world without legs. Since I can't balance myself with my legs so I use my hands to balance myself like a pendulum, but when I'm in the field the stadium packed with the audience just howl one name and that's mine. This hooting is the secret of my enthusiasm towards life.

I was born in a simple family on 3rd Nov1987 in Ohiya (America). I'm only 3'1"tall and weigh 117 pounds, but my courage never let me feel short in height nor disabled. I used a wheelchair. I still remember the day when I was in 7th Grade, it was my second day, the elevator was close and I didn't wait for them to start and went in my class on the second floor through the stairs. Everyone was amazed to see me. The credit for this achievement goes wholly to my mother because in spite of being disabled she never overprotected me. She always believed that I'm capable enough to do my things. My brother played football, so I was inspired by him. I played football far much better than others but even then I was deprived of going on the field. Once National Federation of High School Association tried to stop me by the reverence of their Rules and Regulations but later on I got medical clearance to play. Ohiya High School Athlete Association gave me the permission to participate in the game just like others.

Now when I come to the ground I'm introduced as 'The 2005 Homecoming King' and I have full faith that one should never feel defeated by life in any circumstances, I still remember ,once after match my opponents called me 'Superman'; that was the day when more than 200 people waited for my autograph and for a snap with me. I'm regarded as the 'Musket' of the team.

Irfan Pathan

He was born in Baroda and spent his childhood in the surroundings of Mandvi Jama Masjid. He is a religious person and worships 5 times a day. He belonged to a family with limited income and still he was encouraged to play cricket. He says that concentration, devotion and aggressive is the main requirement of mastering the cricket game. His brother is his biggest critic. He respects all his teachers a lot.

He later on proved himself by making debut to Indian Cricket team with flying colours. He admits that he has become a fast and furious bowler due to his devotion and practice. He loves to sit with his father and talk to him endlessly; he shares a loving bond to his place.

He Says, "Today whatever I have achieved in the world of cricket is also due to the endless support of my maternal uncle, he has always encouraged me and guided me. There were times when we have struggled a lot; we have even stitched our shoes. Success is bound to come when you have faith in your dreams and you are consistent with your efforts."

Sherly Chang - An International Author

I'm from New York and I have been chosen as the finalist in the 'motivational category' of "Next Generation Indy Book Awards 'for this year. This award is given for the publication of the best books which consist of about seventy categories

At the age of eleven months I took my first step to walk but I fell down. Doctors told me that I suffered from arthritis and had lot of swelling on my knees. Doctors were visited now and then but all in vain. After eleven years I was sent to school but my academic performance was not forth appreciable. So I was given 6 months time for preparation and then I was examined, my performance was outstanding after which I was given admission in the 6th standard. Suddenly at the age of 17, I lost my eyesight but all these difficulties never let me lose my hope. Meanwhile I got interested towards writing and I wrote 8 books. Last year my book 'Walking Spirit: Pros and Poems the Spirit Sings' got 7 awards. My books give the inspiration to love life, live it courageously, so that at every step of life we get only success. I personally meet some people who have lost the battle of life.

Klee Dyer

I was born in Hamilton, Alabama. I don't have either my hands or legs. So thank the God and consider yourself lucky if you are in well to do condition. Today at the age of 40 yrs my height is only 40" and I weigh 39 kg. My identity as a fisherman without hands and legs who catches more than 200 fishes at a time is more identical. I have won more than 25 such competitions.

I have 16"imperfect hand on my right; with the help of which I have started doing some of my works on my own. By the age of 15 I started catching fish; in the beginning I was too afraid but soon I learnt to balance myself and explored new methods of fishing. To sail the boat is a hard task; sometimes my friend did this for me. I love **swimming**. *After fishing competitions I'm completely exhausted I go for swimming.*

I already knew that I have **a great passion to learn something**; *so I devoted my time in fishing. I always thought*

only one thing i.e. how can I give my best to whatever work I do. I like to play Baseball in spite of knowing that I'll never be able to become a baseball player still I gave my best efforts to it. I thought of becoming a professional fisherman and I've done it. It is my strong belief that I'm able to do what god wants me to.

Stephen Hawking

The renowned scientist Stephen Hawking says that "One must have an approach to think new and one must try to experiment in life. Remember that you'll achieve success in it. And even if you feel disheartened just think of Thomas Alva Edison who after numerous failures finally succeeded in making the electric bulb". Neither he can speak nor move his hands or legs.

Dr Hawking talks only via expressions. And he converses with the help of a computer connected on his wheelchair. In spite of all such hardships in life he is the role model of many people because to lose, is not in his dictionary. He was the best seller of book called 'A brief history of time'. Even at the age of 65 plus he has not lost his passion towards life. He fulfilled his dream of flying in 'zero gravity'. At present he is a Mathematics professor in Cambridge University.

Miles Hilton

Miles Hilton of Britain is the first Sightless pilot of the world, who has made the record of tour of half of the world with his micro light aircraft. Recently he flew across half of the world in his little aircraft from Begin hill airfield in London. The aim of this audacious journey of Hilton was to collect money for the eradication of the evils of blindness from the developing nations.

Tom Cruise

Tom Cruise, the superstar of Hollywood who gets $25 million (around Rs.113 crore) for a movie. He is an actor who has won the Oscar three times. When he did a show for the first time in the High school he said to his family members that within 10 years he'll earn his Show Business. But within 4 years his movie 'Risky Business' did wonders. Dare to dream and have belief in your own abilities.

Jankhana Shah

She can be called the Chartered Accountant of the new generation. She wants to make the financial system of Mumbai aware about the **money care financial planning.** She was the first and the only women Chartered Financial Planner who is awarded by the Financial Planning Standard by overpowering 150 people. She topped The Chartered Accountants Examination after that she worked as a System Consultant in Bombay Stock Exchange Stock Trading for Daylight Trading. She has opened her own company; her father was a stock broker so money management was a part of her life. After marriage she even did CFP course and at present she is heading her company "Money Care Financial Planning". She says "The three important things related to the generation of money are:- First the physical, mental, emotional, and spiritual wellbeing of a person. Second is the relationship of a person, who remains stuck up in these does not think about his present. And third deciding of an aim and making efforts to achieve it." She also says "Women can do anything if they have the will and determination to do something".

Mohd. Asif Iqbal

I'm not a professional motivator. But I have my own life story to tell you. I had failed four times by the time I reached 5th standard. My teachers view was that I'll never be able to do anything in life. My eyesight was not as good as others; but all this was being ignored. At that time my aunt living in America came to India, she proved to be Godmother to me. She supported my family and took me along with her. By the age of 16 years, I lost my eyesight completely; by then I had completed my High School. Due to family problems I had to return back. None of the colleges gave me admission; after a lot of efforts I got admitted in St. Xavier's College Calcutta. I was the first student to Graduate in Commerce field with brilliant performance. I decided to do MBA for which I gathered study material via net. After clearing the entrance exam I was selected in Symbiosis Centre of Management and Human Resources Development. I finally completed my dream of becoming MBA.

This achievement of mine reached to former president of India Mr. APJ Abdul Kalam and we discussed the necessities of the blind, and found that there's a need to develop a Talking Software of our own. I feel proud that I'm such an MBA who can work on computer, manage the accounts of banks and read the newspaper on my own. I just want to tell people that any kind of physical disability is not a problem but a means to live and fight against life.

Kiran Bedi

The First lady IPS (Indian Police Service) officer of India Kiran Bedi was born on June 9, 1949. Her father Prakash Lal Peshawaria, a landlord in Punjab was determined to educate his four daughters at a time when women were largely limited to do household work only. While studying at the Sacred Heart Convent, Kiran joined the National Cadet Corps (NCC) and took up tennis, a game which her father used to play. After school she went on to study Political Science at the Government College for Women, Amritsar. She loved the subject as she felt it taught her about her role as a citizen of the country.

Kiran excelled at sports particularly tennis. She won the inter-University women's team title and bagged the national title as well as the Asian title in tennis. Bedi says the game taught her the value of hard work, the importance of staying fit and built in her the qualities of fair play, team work, concentration, and the ability to give in that extra bit under stress.

In 1972 Kiran was selected for the Indian Police Service (IPS). Spectators at the 1973 Republic Day Parade were amazed to see a lady at the head of the Police Contingent. The then Prime Minister, Mrs. Indira Gandhi was so impressed that she invited Kiran for breakfast with her the very next day. She never took a step backward fulfilling her duties. She had set many trends by doing extraordinary things as a police officer. In 1977, she put an end to the Akali-Nirankari Sikh riots at India Gate. In 1979, as DCP (West Delhi), she broke up a 200-year-old illicit liquor trade. In 1981 as DCP (Traffic) she controlled traffic during the 1982 Asian Games efficiently. She didn't hesitate to tow away cars and once even challenged the Prime Minister's car for wrong parking near a car repair shop. In 1985, as DCP (headquarters) she ordered 1600 pending promotions to be made in a single day. Standing instructions were issued that if any file was not cleared within three days the person concerned would be called personally to explain the delay. In 1993, as the Inspector General of Asia's biggest jail - the Tihar jail (9100 inmates including 300 women) she turned the unliveable jail into an abode of education, Said Kiran while joining her posting at the jail, "I want to transform this jail into an Ashram within six months". She introduced many classes and programs for the inmates including those on basic education, meditation, yoga besides functions like mushairas, kavi sammelans, dramas and games, for the jail inmates. For her effort to humanise the Tihar jail she was honoured with the Ramon Magsaysay Award in 1994.

The eminent writer, Khushwant Singh, in one of his columns, With Malice towards One And All described Kiran Bedi as "*The gutsiest woman I have ever known*". Not everyone loves this gutsy woman though. Kiran Bedi has been often criticized for being "media-hungry" and controversial. Often, she has been transferred out of offices for trying to turn things around. But despite these minor issues, Kiran Bedi remains one of the most inspiring Indian public figures. Even after retirement, at the age of 62 she is actively engaged to fight with corruption as civil society member.

Christopher Reeve, the Superman

Christopher Reeve, the superman, almost died a decade ago, when on May 27,1995, he fell off from a horse headfirst on the ground, injuring himself badly confining to a ventilator and a wheelchair and finally contemplating suicide. Reeve worked fiercely on his rehabilitation, regained sensation over 70% of his body. He produced miracles by living without ventilator for longer periods, Stunned Doctors by willing himself to move one of his fingers, and legs and arms in water.

The traumatic Reeve was supported throughout by his wife Dana and sons. The relationship with Dana too was a boon. Dana always wanted the family to live as normal as ever. The support from family has been incredible and extra ordinary. Such a tragedy made them close to each other even more.

Their story stands a real testimony to the legendary behaviour of the soul mate and indomitable optimism of the sufferer. Truly, with such blessed relations by your side life naturally becomes heaven even in hellish pains.

Sushil Tudu

After his father's demise, he got a job in a college as peon. Surprisingly, he is a lecturer in the same college in which he was once a peon. He was born to an underprivileged family in Simoldohi village of Dumka district in Bihar (India). But his consistent efforts, zeal to move forward and big thinking encouraged him to do unbelievable and reach the pinnacles of success.

The Blade Runner "Oscar Pistorious"

He is famous as blade runner. This South African athlete doesn't have feet since his birth. Nobody saw him on the track and field but today he has become a sensation in the world of sports. He was not having bones in legs below knees. When he was one year old doctors cut his legs below knees. He started using artificial legs and slowly he started walking then running. He uses carbon fibre made artificial feet. He runs better than, those who have both the legs natural. He has completed 100 meter race in just 10.91 seconds. He qualified for Beijing Olympics in 2008 but due to some technical grounds he was not allowed to participate. In handicapped category he has created many world records. He completed 200 meter race in only 21.58 seconds whereas in 2004 Olympics the gold medal winner took 19.79 seconds to win 200 meter title.

Binod Kumar

He is tailor by vocation, an accomplished painter and a player of international level. Binod of Kolkata doesn't have arms and he learnt writing using his feet. To earn bread and butter he learnt tailoring, embroidery and swimming too. When he was in 8th Standard he started taking more interest in sports and started playing football. Years later he emerged as a champion at college level. He created impact in high jump and swimming also. He keeps on contesting in many state and national level competitions. He won four gold medals in All India swimming competition. He participated in an international event in Britain in 2006 too. He has won gold and silver medals in world games.

Naresh Gulati

Naresh Gulati is from Chandigarh. He failed in high school exams and was almost boycotted by his family and relatives. At the age of 15 he decided to do something different. He started selling clothes and fancy candles on the road side. He started earning and then again joined the school but didn't stop his business of selling candles. He completed computer course and worked with Aptech computers. In 1996 he opened his consultancy firm named as OCA group in which he is rendering services like BPO intelligence, Object next software etc. He has branches in many countries and at the age of 39 his company attained a turnover of Rs. 80 Crores. He inspires thousands of youths by his journey from candle seller to a millionaire.

Anil Agarwal

He is a known name and face in the world. He is close to Mukesh Ambani in terms of wealth accumulation. Recently his wealth was measured close to 69.5 million dollars. You would be shocked to know that he started his business with a small shop from Patna (Bihar) where he used to deal in iron and plastic scrap at a very small level. He formally came into business since 1976 and gradually expanded his business. Today he his heading "VEDANTA Group" and established himself as a big business tycoon.

14

Sunrise Within You

"The New You"

I would like to thank you for your journey with me to this final chapter. You can keep the book in bookshelf and may feel contended that you finished reading it or you can make conscious endeavour to achieve what you dream about and certainly you will realize your dreams if you desperately want to make them happen. Choice is yours!

This story always makes me realize the self worth. Many years ago an estate agent was auctioning the valuable possessions of a rich man. Lastly few unworthy assets remained. The agent brought an old guitar outside the yard and started selling the same. It apparently looked as if guitar was merely a show piece and was of no use. He without any enthusiasm announced to public to bid for it. He said, "Anybody who wants to buy this for Rs.1000/-? ", Nobody raised the hand or voice. He further announced "Okay are you interested to have it for Rs.500/-", still no one came ahead. He kept on reducing the amount and finally the agent reached to an unbelievable price of Re.10/- only.

The moment this price was announced an old man stood up and came in front and said "Would you give me few minutes please?" he held the guitar in his hands, tightened the loose strings, everybody present there was looking at him with curiosity.

He started playing the guitar and within seconds the audiences were hypnotized with the melody. After couple of minutes the old man kept the guitar back on the table and told the estate agent to start the auction afresh.

The Agent started the auction once again with a note "Come on! Who wants to have this amazing and unique guitar, unbelievably many of the persons were keen to buy it. Finally that apparently worthless looking guitar was sold for a huge price of Rs. 50000.

Now why I am narrating this story at the beginning of the final chapter? This is what happens with many of us in our lives. The instrument, nobody was interested in having all most for no cost but finally the same was sold out for an extra ordinary price. I have seen many humans who in spite of having a great potential never realize their real worth and struggle all through their lives. If you under rate yourself no one is going to rate you high. You are required to understand your real worth and presenting yourself in best of the manner so that this world can know who you actually are?

"The first step towards success is identifying your own strengths."

We all have natural talents, skills and potentials. Either we are ignorant about them or we don't use them. What you need is, to re-discover yourself. Most of the people in the world die without using their potentials fully and I don't want you to be one of them.

"It's Never too late to become the person,
you have always dreamt of being."

- Robin Sharma

Your Intrinsic Value:

I saw one of my friends who is an accomplished trainer starting his seminars by holding up Rs 1000/-note and asking participants, "Who would like this note?" Invariably most hands were raised. Then he crumpled the note and repeated the question again... "Everybody still wants it". Then, he dropped it on the ground and crumpled it with his shoes. "Now who still wants it?" he asks. Nobody changed his or her mind. They wanted it despite the dirt. They wanted it because of its worth has not been sullied by the dirt.

Surely, this is very valuable lesson. No matter what was done to the currency note, people still wanted it because it did not decrease in value. It was still worth Rs 1000/- Ditto for us human beings! Many times in our lives, we are dropped, crumpled, and ground into the dirt by the decisions we make and the circumstances that come our way. No matter what has happened or what will happen, you will never lose your worth if you are aligned to the path of truth.

The worth of the sullied note does not diminish because it carried the proof of being a currency that was recognized by everybody as having the stated worth. Similarly, we have to confirm our worth by proving our values intact... a fact that is proven by our responses to different situations. If our actions are appropriate then our values are confirmed and our character will be considered worthy.

Personal worthiness is a value we can attach to ourselves by ensuring that our walk is aligned to the same values that we talk about. Too often, we talk about lofty values and indulge in lowly deeds. Too often, we find excuses to justify the most reprehensible of actions.

Too often, we diminish our own worth by compromising on our values. Too often, we indulge in the various practices that we have publicly condemned.

Have a Clear Vision

"Your mind has the power to give you everything you want. But it can only do that if it's getting clear, bright, intense, focused signals."

– Anthony Robins

The medical science in many of its researches has proved that the mind is most miraculous body part a human being has. Unless we use it to its best it's not going to create those miracles. Why are we talking of thinking ahead and having a clear vision? Unless we have a clear vision for years to come, we can't align today's action with what we wish to achieve in future. We must learn from companies like Sony & Microsoft whose research team is ready with the products to be launched 25 years from now. They have a clear vision that what kind of products would be needed in coming 25 years and they have already invented them. We should be proactive enough to predict the future and making ourselves ready to deal with them. Most people change themselves only when world changes and it becomes inevitable for them to get changed.

"Achievers never lose their focus. They just keep their eyes on the big picture."

Search the Mission of Your Life

I generally ask one question in my seminars. What is the mission of your life? Where do you want to see yourself at the age of 60? When a child is born he doesn't know about life and gradually he grows to teenage, starts dreaming for college life. Once he reaches to college, starts dreaming of higher education or job. Now he is in job he thinks of getting married. After marriage he dreams for a child. Later on he starts feeling as a responsible father for upbringing of his children. Once he attains the 50 he stops thinking for his growth. I would like to ask all these people (remember they are in majority) what was the single purpose for which they lived? What is their accomplishment? Most people in this world have no well defined or worthy purpose of living.

I remember amazing lines of Robin Sharma here, **"When you were born, you cried while the world rejoiced. You should live your life in such a way that when you die the world cries while you rejoice".**

"If a man hasn't discovered something that he can die for, he is not fit to live."
- Martin Luther King, Jr.

Learn to Handle Complacency

"That which is achieved the most, still has the whole of its future yet to be achieved."
- Lao Tsu

I have witnessed people, big tycoons, industrialists, sportsmen reaching on pinnacle and then stop. They start to get easy and ultimately they lose what got them to this position.

Going back to the comfort zone proves to be fatal. The moment you go in comfort zone you stop growing, you stop working passionately, you stop adding value to your actions. The day you stop confronting with problems and challenges, you have stopped growing. Someone correctly said "life is like riding a bicycle either you ride or you fall. You are either growing or perishing. The life can't stand still.

I was listening to the renowned film director of Indian film industry 'Prakash Jha' who recently came up with a movie featuring Amitabh Bachhan in the lead role. While replying to the question asked "How he felt working with the star of the century Amitabh Bachhan? He said "I feel inspired the way I see Amitabh working, his passion, zeal and energy at the age of 67 years is mind blowing. I can see in him a lot of hunger for his work which is generally seen in a new comer", simply amazing and that's how achievers are born.

We will have plenty of time to sleep once we die, Let us live our life to the fullest and give out hundred percent.

Pain of Discipline Vs. Pain of Regret

Most people struggle with mediocrity and fail to do well in life because somewhere they avoided hard work, discipline or consistency. Many people want to do great things, they start up with lots of enthusiasm and vigour but very soon they give up. Most students feel motivated and start studying with full energy and a week later they come back on the same lazy track. Having that discipline to perform at highest level is bit painful and most of us fail to carry disciplined efforts with consistency. Later when you realize it is too late and you feel that the pain of discipline was nothing as compared to this pain of regret of doing nothing. Discipline is something so powerful that makes you doing those things which you dream of doing but don't feel like doing.

George Bernard Shaw was asked on deathbed, "What would you do if you get another chance to live?" He replied, "I would like to be the person I could have become but could not become."

Have a Personal Diary

Maintaining and writing personal diary is as good as having a best companion with you every time. The moment you get an idea you should write it. You may write your goals, targets and habits you want to improve upon. If you have something in your mind which constantly makes you worried, write them down in your diary you will feel relaxed. Most of our targets we keep in our mind and our mind being so manipulative keep on changing them according to the situation. When you write them down, they become self commitments and that constantly reminds you what is there still to be achieved.

Medical science in its researches has revealed that writing personal diary on daily basis helps you keeping fit your health, immune system and your attitude too.

Be Loyal to Yourself

I often feel and say, "If we are not loyal to ourselves we can never be loyal to anybody else in our life". We make promises to ourselves and keep on breaking or postponing them. We break commitments and we actually cheat ourselves. If you break your own commitment to yourself, you should feel pain inside otherwise later it would become a habit of yours. Give yourself a commitment, stand firm to it and don't sit quiet until you fulfil it.

Learn from a Child

I wonder, when we were children, we were very natural and we gradually became unnatural. We forgot learning of our childhood. I would like to remind you something here. Learn to keep yourself busy like a child, stay happy without any reason, share your possessions, don't hit people, Say sorry when you hurt somebody, clean up your own mess, put things back where you found them and play fair. Bring these changes back to your life and you will see amazing results happening to you and to your daily life around.

Be the Best Dreamer

Everyone dreams. What you dream is your choice. Your dreams shape your destiny. Believe me if you chase your dreams your dreams will chase the reality. I have experienced that dreams come true. Many of my dreams, which I saw while sleeping and which were apparently far from my reach, came true. It's not an eternal power given to me by god, but it's natural. All of us can predict and chase the future. You should have faith on your dreams, others may ridicule you for your dreams, don't bother and keep thinking and working towards your dreams. Your dreams should grow along with your progress. Keep the size of your dreams that big which can inculcate a sense of passion and challenge within you to attain them in real.

"The size of your dreams will determine how big a person you will become."

- Robert H. Schuller.

Focus on Action not Results

I am very impressed with words of Mahatma Gandhi which go like this, "It's the action, not the fruit of the action, that's important. You have to do the right thing. It may not be in your power, may not be in your time, that there'll be any fruit. But that doesn't mean you stop doing the right thing. You may never know what results come from your action. But if you do nothing, there will be no result."

"Nobody can do everything but everyone can do something."

I'm only one. But still, I am one. I cannot do everything, but still I can do something. And because I cannot do everything, I will not refuse to do the something that I can do.

- Edward Everett Hale

One Step at a time & every step a master stroke

Robin Sharma, my favourite author observed "It got me thinking about the importance of showing up fully at work – giving the fullness of your brilliance and playing full out. Be wildly passionate about your actions. Be breathtakingly committed to your projects and opportunities. Be a rock star in whatever you do each day to put bread on your table. Work gives meaning to our lives. It influences our self-worth and the way we perceive our place under the sun. Being spectacularly great at your work promotes personal respect, excitement and just makes your life a lot more interesting. Good things happen to people who do good things. When you bring your highest talents and deepest devotion to the work you do, what you are really doing is setting yourself up for a richer, happier and more fulfilling experience of living".

Dr. Martin Luther King Jr. also observed – "If a man is called to be a street sweeper, he should sweep street even as Michelangelo painted, or as Beethoven composed music or Shakespeare wrote poetry. He should sweep streets so well that all the hosts of heaven and earth will pause to say, 'here lived a great street sweeper who did his job well'."

Follow the Kaizen Principle

The Japanese term 'Kaizen' means "continuous improvement", Let us learn and improve on regular basis. Norman cousin once said, "The tragedy of life is not death, but what we let die inside us while we live." Those who are in the process of continuous improvement are always ahead of others. Don't let a single day of your life go without making yourself enriched with new learning, experience and value additions. Don't stop growing and expanding. Don't become a person who dies at 25 years of age and get buried at 75 years of age.

Practice the Patience

"The Art of Patience is not much about how long one can wait, but it is about how one behaves while waiting."

Patience is something which is becoming a rare personality attribute in the new generation. Patience doesn't mean sitting quietly and waiting for something good to happen. Patience means carrying out your actions religiously without losing calmness and avoiding desperation. Patience is the key to peace and happiness. It helps you accumulating energy and using it to the fullest for right purposes. Getting impatient leads to irritation, which causes imbalance to your thoughts and finally efficiency deteriorates. If you are impatient it is visible through your behaviour too.

If you practice patience you stay cool, balanced, efficient and well behaved person.

"Genius is eternal patience."
- Michelangelo

Get Rid of Your Fears

We have been given an environment where we have learned to be sceptical and suspicious. We avoid taking risks and trying new ways. We believe in orthodox styles. Out of many fears, the fear of failure is most dangerous and destructive. When you take an action, the result is unknown rather it's out of your control. Thinking negative about the outcome or not taking action because you are afraid of getting failed is not going to help you anyway. It's better to try and fail instead of not trying it at all. Every failure is going to add some lesson or experience to your life. You have to get rid of your deep rooted fears and unleash your real self.

Going Beyond...

Most of us have self imposed limitations and preconceived notions. Don't hold yourself back, Move ahead with full energy and vigour and you will see first two letters of word 'impossible' disappearing. Use your free time in gaining new knowledge or learning new things. You have no time, is a self imposed limitation which helps you becoming an obsolete product. Impossible is now a personal opinion, what you think impossible is being done by somebody in this world.

Take Charge

You have to take responsibility for your action. You are the pilot of your airplane. You are responsible for your destiny. Blaming others or your circumstances for your low performance is not going to help you anyways. You are responsible to take your decisions. You are a person, who is internally driven and not a puppet! You have a strong will power. You are capable of making good judgments. You are strong enough to bring desired changes to your life. You are capable of fighting with adverse situations and come up more strongly. You are the captain of your soul because the steering of your life is in total control of yours.

Make Positive Attitude Your Way of Life

You can attain anything and make everything look simple if you have positive attitude in life. You need to have positive attitude towards your work, your relationship, your health, your future and everything you confront with. This positive attitude will give you lots of energy to carry out your efforts with higher intensity. It will make you feel happy. Life will be more fun. You will visualize positive outcome of all the events which in fact will bring better outcome than your expectations. Your resistance to fight to odd circumstances will grow to unbelievable degree. Remember 80% of the outcome of your life is dominated by your attitude. The moment you perceive the outcome of an action being positive, you start performing to your peak. Be the best, Always.

Mind your Thoughts

Your Thoughts build your life. You are a person what you think across the day. Your life is made of number of days you live and quality of your thoughts is going to determine the quality of your life. Each negative or perverted thought somewhere add virus to your mind and takes out positive energy. If we are not happy with somebody, cursing that person in your thoughts makes you more unstable and you may not focus on your priorities. What type of thoughts you inculcate in your mind is entirely your choice. Hence I say what kind of life you are going to lead is also entirely your choice. Your life follows your thoughts.

Also spend some time regularly in constructive thinking about yourself and your future. We generally keep too busy with our daily routines and hardly introspect. Many successful companies have recommended their executives to compulsorily spend some time in thinking during work, keeping mobile phone and other gadgets aside. It really works. Most of us fail to use the most powerful possession "The Mind" by not thinking in a structured and constructive manner.

Develop Productive Habits

We all have some hobbies. I ask you to have hobbies which are productive in nature, which take your worries away and you feel passionate while getting involved into that. You must develop a habit of reading regularly. Forget about news papers. Read good journals or books which enrich your knowledge and make you feel confident. If you read good books your vision gets more clarity & your horizon expands. Reading makes you a person who is fit in all communities and circles. You never become obsolete, you never feel suffocated and a good amount of self contentment is attained. Your productive hobbies should also include playing some outdoor sports. Getting involved with productive habits in your spare time keeps you fit, fresh, energetic, inspired and positive.

Be a Strong Leader

You must develop a leader within you. I don't expect everyone to be a public leader but having leadership traits in your personality makes you stand different from the crowd. Leader who is a mentor and guide to people, people have faith in him, he leads through example and many more. Leadership starts with self then it goes further. A person who can't guide himself or herself can't think of leading others. The leader has to be self disciplined and self motivated. The leader is a visionary and able to see what others can't see. You as a leader take charge of your circumstances, you take the ownership of your life and you are not afraid of taking risks. If you develop that leader inside you, you will be the first beneficiary of it. Having leadership skills helps you achieving your goals much faster and with higher scales.

"Well focused, self confident leadership is what turns a vision into reality."

Relations – Soul of Your Life

You are nobody without your relations. The contentment in your life is directly proportionate to quality of your relationships. You work hard in your studies, in your job or business to make your future better. Imagine this future without your family or imagine it without sweetness in your relations. You will find this success to be worthless. You need a strong bond with your friends and a good social network. Without these your achievements are incomplete. Your friends and relatives make your accomplishments worth mentioning. Be friendly and caring, don't do over commitments but try to deliver better than what you promised for, add value to peoples' life. Be a good listener and show interest in people you meet. Don't take your near and dear ones for granted, courtesy should be integral part of your behaviour//r and always try to get the tag of trustworthiness from your friends.

Have an Ideal

I imagine my life to be shaky and very ordinary, if I wouldn't have had certain ideals in my life. A person who inspires you through his or her action, accomplishments and philosophy should be your ideal. If you make somebody your ideal, that becomes a source of inspiration for you. If you want to become like your ideal, you observe minutely and try to learn many things from your ideal. Having ideal in our life, gives a sense of clear direction to us. We may have many ideals. For me Mr. Anil Jain, my senior partner is an ideal as a perfect chartered accountant and Mr. Nirmal Parekh a great motivator is another ideal to me as a prolific trainer. I also take Mr. Amitabh Bachhan as my role model for being a wonderful human.

Power of Enthusiasm

There will be good and bad times in your life. Don't let your enthusiasm fade. This enthusiasm should reflect from your body language, action and speech. Your enthusiasm in your action enhances the intensity. Create a vocabulary of a successful, positive, inspiring individual. Be passionate in your speech and express your enthusiasm with your words. ***The energy of the words that you speak is a powerful force that is creative.***

Achieving Significance in Life

If you want to achieve significance in your life, ask following questions to yourself and then decide the course of action:

1. How do I want myself to be different?
2. How do I want my family to be different?
3. How do I want my profession to be different?
4. How do I want my relationship to be different?
5. How do I want my society to be different?
6. How do I want this world to be different?

Celebrate Your Life

You should celebrate because you are alive. You should celebrate because you are destined to be a human. The nature has gifted us the power to smile and laugh. Your success has no meaning if it can't make you smile. Learn to enjoy and celebrate small achievements and occasions of your life. We keep on postponing our happiness to future moments, that once I will achieve this I will be happy but that never happens. Make that fun and masti (joy) an integral part of your daily life. Laugh like you will never have another chance to laugh. For me every day is a festival and a matter of celebration because the god has given me one more day to live. Stay happy and make the journey of your life full of fun.

You are Lucky & Blessed

If you woke up today with no pain you are luckier than most. If you have never known the dangers of war, loneliness of prison, or hunger, you are better off than 500 million people in the world. If you can go to your mosque, church, or temple or follow your beliefs without persecution, you are luckier than more than 3 million people on this planet. If your basic needs are covered, you are richer than 75% of the rest of the world. If you even have some savings, you are part of the 10% of the most prosperous people in the world. If you saw your parents grow old together, you are almost unique. If you smile and appreciate life, you are lucky because lots of people can, but they don't. If you have someone whose hand you can hold, or can hug, or even just a shoulder to touch, be happy, you will never be lonely. Never forget to thank god for these blessings.

Good Bye.....

Lord, I want your heart to be in my heart. For in You I come alive, moving ahead from boring death to exciting life!

In Your promises, I will move from discouragement to hope.

In Your pardon, I will move from shame to glory.

In Your power, I will move from weakness to strength.

In Your providence, I will move from failure to success!

Thank You, Lord.

(Courtesy: "Success is never Ending, Failure is never final" by Robert H. Schuller)

Amen

About the Author

CA Pritam Kumar Goswami

He completed his Chartered Accountancy course from New Delhi and later qualified DISA (Diploma in Information System Audit). He has qualified EXCEL (From JCI University, USA). He has also done Post Graduate Diploma in Business Administration (HR) From Symbiosis Centre for Distance Learning, Pune. He became International Training Fellow # 148 of JCI Trainings USA in 2010.

He was Born and brought up in Kota, Rajasthan (India)

He is a practicing Chartered Accountant and acting as a partner in ASAP & Associates having offices in Kota, Jaipur & New Delhi. He is a Director at CICA (Career Institute of Commerce & Accounts) which imparts coaching/education to Commerce students at mass level. He has been into teaching for past 15 years and till now he has mentored more than 10000 students across India. He is considered to be a fire brand ace trainer (Motivator & Life Management Coach) at international level. In last

12 years he has conducted more than 1000 seminars for Junior Chamber International, NGO's, Corporate and Educational Institutions in India and abroad. He has contributed many articles in magazines and news papers. Apart from this book he has also authored a book on Cost Accounting for CA Students.

He being an International Trainer has conducted his seminars in various International Conferences in Nagano & Osaka (Japan), Bussan (Korea), Singapore, Manila (Philippines), Hong Kong, Brussels (Belgium), Hammamet (Tunisia) & in many other countries. He has visited more than 25 countries for social and training commitments.

He has been a social activist and has been involved with many social organizations. He has been a member of Junior Chambers International (JCI) since 1997. He has been imparting invaluable lessons of life & skills through his programs like "Positive Mental Attitude, Work Life Balance, Stress Management, Inter-personal Skills, Leadership, Team-Building,

Creativity, Public Speaking, Presentational Skills, Passion & Motivation, Effective Parenting, Time-Management etc."

Under his leadership in the year 2005 & 2006 his local chapter JCI Kota Dynamic won two International Awards. He held the position of State President of JCI India in 2008, National Director (Business) in 2009 & National Coordinator of International Affairs in 2012.

He is actively associated with Rotary Club and local branch of Institute of Chartered Accountants of India (ICAI). He was the Chairman of Kota branch of ICAI in 2002. He is involved in Social projects of Blood Donation, Active Citizen Movement & Tripti- the Food Project.

He has been delivering talks on FM Radio. He guides students and people through Personal Counselling.

He has been honoured with the following awards:-

- By Ishaan Institute of Management and Technology, Greater Noida in 2005 for his appreciable contribution in academics.
- Ravi Puruskar in 2006 for being the best trainer in Rajasthan by JCI
- Eklavya Award in 2009 for his outstanding contribution in the field of Training & mentoring by JCI India Zone V.
- Best Member & Best President of Local chapter of JCI in 2005 & 2006 in Rajasthan.
- Best National officer of JCI India in 2009.
- By Kota branch of ICAI for outstanding contribution as Chairman in 2009 and 2012.
- By Rotary Club Kota in 2008 and Rotary Club Kota North in 2012 for outstanding social and professional contribution.
- Life Time Achievement award by Junior Chamber International in 2012 for outstanding contribution at State level.

He is a person who maintains Self-discipline and consistency in his daily life, one who follows his own guidelines to make his life better. He is self-motivated and passionate for whatever work he takes up.

He believes in – ***"Be different and make the Difference"***.

www.ingramcontent.com/pod-product-compliance
Lightning Source LLC
La Vergne TN
LVHW042348150826
845671LV00002B/63

* 9 7 9 8 8 9 4 7 5 7 3 3 9 *